BETTER BUSINESS BUREAU®

Insider's Guide to Success

D0580156

Buying a Franchise

The Better Business Bureau

with Mard Naman

thePlanningshop

Palo Alto, California

Better Business Bureau Buying a Franchise: Insider's Guide to Success
©2007 by Rhonda Abrams. Published by The Planning Shop™

ISBN 13: 978-1-933895-01-7
ISBN: 1-933895-01-2
PCN: 2007928725

Managing Editor: Maggie Canon
Project Editor: Mireille Majoor
Cover and interior design: Diana Van Winkle

Bulk Discounts and Special Sales
Better Business Bureaus, corporate purchasing, colleges, consultants:
The Planning Shop offers special volume discounts as well as supplemental materials for BBBs, universities, business schools, and corporate training. Contact:
    info@PlanningShop.com
    or call 650-289-9120

The Planning Shop™ is a division of Rhonda, Inc., a California corporation.

Cover photos © iStockphoto.com/Sean Locke, Julie de Leseleuc, Phil Date, Dragan Trifunovic

"This publication is designed to provide accurate and authoritative information in regard to the subject matter covered. It is sold with the understanding that the publisher and author are not engaged in rendering legal, accounting, or other professional services. If legal advice or other expert assistance is required, seek the services of a competent professional."
— *from a Declaration of Principles, jointly adopted by a committee of the American Bar Association and a committee of publishers*

Distributed by National Book Network

Printed in Canada

10 9 8 7 6 5 4 3 2

A Message from BBB President Steven Cole

B uying a franchise is one of the biggest financial commitments a person can make. Franchises can cost thousands, if not hundreds of thousands, of dollars. Having a trusted source to guide you through the process of selecting a franchise means you'll find one that is reputable and fits your personal and financial goals. That source is the *Better Business Bureau Buying a Franchise: Insider's Guide to Success*.

Better Business Bureau Buying a Franchise: Insider's Guide to Success walks you through every step of acquiring a franchise—how to research and evaluate different franchise opportunities, how much franchises cost, how to be sure the franchise you're interested in is legitimate and has a proven track record, what you need to know about the all-important disclosure document called the Uniform Franchise Offering Circular (UFOC), and what you can—and can't—negotiate in the franchise agreement.

When you're investigating franchises, you'll come into contact with many different kinds of businesses. The BBB fosters fair and honest relationships between businesses and consumers, which means that during any step of this process, you can check up on the franchises you're considering. And the BBB provides extensive services for entrepreneurs, including free Reliability Reports, arbitration services, and best-practices standards, to name just a few. For more information, see page viii or check our website at *www.bbb.org*.

This book will help you navigate the process of buying a franchise. We interviewed experts from among our 400,000 BBB members to find out what you need to know, which pitfalls to avoid, and the best resources to use when making the decision to buy a franchise. The expertise and experience of BBB members provide insights you won't find in any other book.

Steven J. Cole
President and CEO
Council of Better Business Bureaus

According to a recent Gallup poll, 85 percent of Americans prefer to do business with a BBB member. In this book, you'll get the same reliability, dependability, and impartiality that consumers have come to expect from the BBB.

What Is the Better Business Bureau?

Whether you're checking out the reputation of a national franchise, need help resolving a dispute with a local business, or want to find out more about a charity, the Better Business Bureau (BBB) supplies you, as consumer or businessperson, with the information you need.

With more than 150 independent local bureaus across the United States and Canada, BBBs contribute in a wide variety of ways to their communities. Local bureaus compile Reliability Reports, track and respond to complaints about businesses, arbitrate disputes, maintain websites where consumers can research companies and learn about local issues and scams, and work to encourage businesses to commit to delivering goods and services with integrity.

With consumers' help, the BBB is usually the first national group to learn of problems in specific industries. The BBB was on the front lines of the automobile "lemon law" debate in the 1980s. Individual states got on board, and with the BBB's assistance, enacted "lemon laws" to protect consumers who purchase defective motor vehicles.

Through the BBB's national website (*www.bbb.org*) and local bureaus, the BBB helps consumers determine whether companies and services are reputable. The BBB does this in many ways:

1. Consumer complaints (see page x for how to file a complaint)

2. Reliability Reports (see page viii for how to access these reports)

3. Dispute Resolution

4. Code and Performance Standards

5. Online Business Reliability Certification Program

6. Articles and Videos

Dispute Resolution

The Better Business Bureau offers a binding arbitration program to people and/or businesses in need of marketplace dispute resolution. The BBB provides a professionally trained arbitrator who listens to both sides, weighs the evidence, and makes a decision about the dispute. (While most bureaus provide this as a complimentary service, some charge non-member companies.)

Code of Advertising

Protecting consumers from deceptive and unfair advertising is at the heart of the BBB's mission. The BBB publishes a Code of Advertising that all members must adopt. The directives contain very specific rules, including when it is and is not appropriate to use terms such as *free*, *factory direct*, and *list price*.

What the BBB Isn't

1. The BBB does not protect its own. The organization produces reports on, and conducts investigations into, both member and non-member companies.

2. The BBB is not a government agency. It is a private, non-profit organization funded by membership dues and other support.

Online Business Reliability Certification Program

For companies selling products and services online, the BBB provides an online certification program. The **Online Reliability Seal** means that a company is a BBB member, has met the BBB's Code of Advertising, has been in business for at least one year, and is committed to dispute resolution to address customer complaints.

Articles and Videos

The BBB website (*www.bbb.org*) contains more than 800 free articles from "Work at Home Schemes" to "Choosing an Assisted Living Facility." For a complete list of articles, go to *www.bbb.org/alerts/tips.asp*.

The BBB also produces educational videos on various businesses, services, and products. The content is developed through extensive research, interviews with industry leaders, and reviews of consumer complaints. For a complete list of videos, go to *www.bbbvideo.com*. The videos are for purchase but are also available at most libraries.

The BBB is supported by more than 400,000 local business members nationwide. It is dedicated to fostering fair and honest relationships between businesses and consumers, instilling consumer confidence, and contributing to an ethical business environment.

BBB Membership Requirements

To be a member of the Better Business Bureau, a company must:

1. Be in business at least six months

2. Pay annual dues, determined by the size of the company

3. Meet all relevant licensing and bonding requirements

4. Promptly respond to all customer complaints and make a good faith effort to resolve all complaints

5. Cooperate with the BBB to eliminate any underlying causes of customer complaints

6. Comply with decisions rendered through the BBB's arbitration programs

7. Adhere to BBB standards in its advertising and selling practices

8. Agree to use the BBB name and/or logo only in the manners specifically authorized by the BBB

9. Support the principles and purposes of the BBB and not engage in any activities that reflect adversely on the Bureau

10. Supply appropriate background information to the BBB

11. Have no unsatisfactory reports in its Bureau's service area

12. Cooperate with the BBB's efforts to promote voluntary self-regulation within the company's industry

13. Be free from any government action that demonstrates a failure of the company to support the principles and purposes of the BBB

How to Check on a Company

When you are determining which franchise to acquire, the BBB can help you investigate a company's past performance to find out whether any complaints have been lodged against it. This process is called a Reliability Report (*www.bbb.org/reports.asp*), and in 2006, the system offered Reports on nearly 3 million U.S. and Canadian companies.

Reliability Reports list each company's name, address, phone number, fax, and contact person's name and email address. They also show if, and how, the company has resolved past disputes and if any actions have been taken against the company and/or its principals by government agencies. The BBB posts three years' worth of complaints for each company.

Complaints cover advertising issues, contract disputes, billing/collection issues, operational practices, product problems, and a category labeled "undefined issues." For example, one company's Reliability Report contained the following information: "This company has an unsatisfactory record due to its failure to respond to one or more complaints from consumers. The Bureau processed a total of 415 complaints about this company in the last three years; 191 in the past year."

You may search for information on a company that isn't yet in the BBB database. The Bureau generally waits until it receives three inquiries before starting a file on a particular company.

If you don't have access to a computer, you can receive a hard copy of a company's Reliability Report by calling your local BBB.

Information, Please

The BBB received nearly 102 million requests for assistance and 49.1 million requests for Reliability Reports in 2006, a 19 percent increase over 2005. The largest number of requests concerned:

1. Mortgage brokers: 1,357,199

2. Roofing contractors: 1,339,490

3. General contractors: 1,150,769

4. Movers: 1,109,342

5. New car dealers: 897, 929

6. Work-at-home companies: 753,306

7. Home builders: 721,458

8. Construction & remodeling services: 702,473

9. Auto repair & service shops: 691,793

10. Plumbing contractors: 602,741

How to File a Complaint

W hen a company says something in its ads that isn't true or sells you a product that doesn't work and refuses to fix the problem even after you've complained, what can you do? Some of us would stew about it, maybe tell a few friends, and refuse to ever do business with that company again. But you *can* take action (and help other consumers) by filing a formal complaint at *http://complaint.bbb.org*.

The BBB launches investigations, sometimes in conjunction with law enforcement agencies, whenever:

1. There is a pattern of inquiries or complaints about one particular company, and especially when there is a large number of inquiries or complaints

2. A company's offer is unusual or suspicious, is large in dollar value, or affects a vulnerable group (senior citizens, for example)

3. A company's principals will not cooperate with or provide the BBB with requested information

Because of this complaint system, the BBB is often the first organization to know about potential scams and troubling trends in particular industries. When a scam develops in one part of the country, the news travels quickly between BBB offices in the U.S., Canada, and Puerto Rico, and these offices, in turn, alert the media and the public. The BBB handled more than 1.2 million consumer complaints in 2006 and conducted nearly 11,000 investigations.

Once you've filed a complaint, the BBB will send a letter to the offending company to confirm that you truly are/were a customer and to get their side of the story. If you want additional information or need assistance with a complaint, please contact your local BBB, visit the BBB website (*www.bbb.org*), or call (703) 276-0100.

The Top Recipients of Consumer Complaints in 2006*:

1. Cellular phone services & supplies: 29,237

2. New car dealers: 23,380

3. Internet shopping services: 18,054

4. Furniture stores: 16,461

5. Banks: 15,250

6. Collection agencies: 14,463

7. Internet service providers: 14,353

8. Cable TV, CATV, & satellite: 13,394

9. Telephone companies: 12,371

10. Used car dealers: 11,225

* The BBB AUTO LINE program is counted separately. It handled 37, 434 complaints involving automobile warranty claims in 2006.

Note also that these figures represent actual complaints, not the larger number of requests for assistance and requests for Reliability Reports received in 2006.

About The Planning Shop

The Planning Shop, a nationally recognized publisher of quality books for entrepreneurs, is proud to publish the Better Business Bureau Insider's Guides to Success. The first three titles in the series are: *Buying a Home*, *Starting an eBay Business*, and *Buying a Franchise*.

The Planning Shop, located in Palo Alto, California, specializes in creating business resources for entrepreneurs. The Planning Shop's books and other products are based on years of real-world experience, and they share secrets and strategies from CEOs, investors, lenders, and seasoned business experts.

The Planning Shop's books have been adopted at more than five hundred business schools, colleges, and universities. Hundreds of thousands of entrepreneurs and students have used The Planning Shop's books to launch businesses and create business plans in every industry.

CEO Rhonda Abrams founded The Planning Shop in 1999. An experienced entrepreneur, Rhonda has started three successful companies. Her background gives her a real-life understanding of the challenges facing people who set up and run their own businesses. Rhonda is the author of numerous books on entrepreneurship, and her first, *The Successful Business Plan: Secrets & Strategies,* has sold more than 600,000 copies and was acclaimed by *Forbes* and *Inc.* magazines as one of the top ten business books for entrepreneurs. Rhonda also writes the nation's most widely circulated column on entrepreneurship and small business.

Successful Business Strategies appears on USAToday.com and Inc.com and in more than one hundred newspapers each week. She is also the small business columnist for Yahoo Finance.

The Planning Shop's other lines of books include:

The **Successful Business series**, assisting entrepreneurs and business students in planning and growing businesses:

- *The Successful Business Plan: Secrets & Strategies*

- *Six-Week Start-Up*

- *What Business Should I Start?*

- *The Owner's Manual for Small Business*

The **In A Day series**, enabling entrepreneurs to tackle a critical business task and *Get it done right, get it done fast*™

- *Business Plan In A Day*

- *Winning Presentation In A Day*

- *Trade Show In A Day*

- *Finding an Angel Investor In A Day*

Books published by The Planning Shop are available in bookstores across the country and online at *www.PlanningShop.com.*

Table of Contents

A Message from BBB President Steven Cole iii

What Is the Better Business Bureau? iv

How to Check on a Company viii

How to File a Complaint.. x

About The Planning Shop xii

SECTION 1: FOLLOW YOUR DREAM TO FRANCHISE OWNERSHIP

CHAPTER 1: What a Good Franchise Can Do for You 4

CHAPTER 2: The Wide, Wide World of Franchises 10

CHAPTER 3: The Franchise Players 19

SECTION 2: ARE YOU A FRANCHISE PERSON?

CHAPTER 4: Who's the Boss? 26

CHAPTER 5: What Kind of Franchise Person Are You? 30

CHAPTER 6: It Takes a Village 37

SECTION 3: FIND THE RIGHT FRANCHISE FOR YOU

CHAPTER 7: Seventeen Steps to Franchise Ownership 42

CHAPTER 8: Assess Franchise Opportunities 51

CHAPTER 9: Where to Search for Franchise Opportunities 61

SECTION 4: HOW MUCH WILL IT COST?

CHAPTER 10: Cost Overview 76

CHAPTER 11: How Much Will You Make? 90

SECTION 5: THE UFOC AND FRANCHISE AGREEMENT

CHAPTER 12: The Uniform Franchise Offering Circular (UFOC) 94

CHAPTER 13: The Franchise Agreement 102

SECTION 6: DUE DILIGENCE

CHAPTER 14: Interview Other Franchisees 122

CHAPTER 15: Interview the Franchisor 131

SECTION 7: FINANCE YOUR FRANCHISE

CHAPTER 16: Start-up Funding 144

CHAPTER 17: Explore Your Financing Options 148

CHAPTER 18: Write the Franchise Business Plan 161

CHAPTER 19: Welcome to the World of Franchise Ownership 167

SECTION 8: RESOURCES

To research potential franchises and any complaints about them 172

Franchise trade organizations 172

Franchise research and analysis 174

Help from experienced businesspeople 175

Websites 177

Print directories 179

Trade shows, conferences, and seminars 181

Magazines 183

Glossary of Common Franchise Terms 185

Sample Franchise Agreement (Excerpt) 189

Index 207

Acknowledgments 213

Ready-Made Business Model

"The absolute biggest benefit of franchises is for people who have always wanted to own their own business but don't feel they have the experience or knowledge to do it by themselves. There's a lot of stuff that goes on in business that's not so glamorous—processes and procedures like staffing and financial models, budgeting, paying bills, and on down the list. Franchises have the business model figured out."

Todd Cameron, BBB member,
Subway franchise owner, and venture capitalist,
Columbus, Ohio

Follow *your* Dream *to* Franchise Ownership

What a Good Franchise Can Do for You

F ranchisors—at their best—offer an excellent opportunity for those who want to own their own businesses. The best franchises provide you with a proven product or service, a well-known brand name, advertising and marketing, training and support, and a proven method of running a business. They are true partners with you in your success. These franchises are turnkey solutions to help you get up and running fast and be successful.

Franchisors—at their worst—prey on the desires of those who want to own their own businesses. They make money from selling franchises, rather than from helping franchisees build their businesses. They may offer little or no training, provide little or no advertising or marketing, require you to pay inflated prices for supplies, or allow others to encroach on your territory.

QUICK TIP

Franchisee or Franchisor?

When you acquire a franchise, you become a *franchisee*. You've purchased the right to sell the products or services of a company and use their name for a specified length of time. The company that sold you the rights to use its name and sell its products or services is called the *franchisor*. Domino's Pizza, Subway, and Jiffy Lube are all franchisors.

Through research and due diligence, you can find a reputable opportunity that is right for you—one that provides you with the level of support and guidance that *you* need, offers a product or service that will work in *your* market, that fits *your* interests and working style, and that you can afford.

In the best cases, franchising is a win-win situation for both sides. As a franchisee, you get:

- An established brand name for your business
- The marketing muscle of a parent company
- A tried-and-true business plan
- A proven business model
- Combined purchasing power
- Training
- Administrative support
- Financing (potentially)
- To be part of a larger company and yet be self-employed

In turn, the franchisor gets:

- A way to expand their business rapidly
- Committed business *owners* (not just employees) to run their locations
- Additional capital investment from the franchisees into their locations
- Income to help them market the company and improve their products and services
- Income from franchise fees and royalties

Are You Really "Buying" a Franchise?

Even though the name of this book is the *Better Business Bureau Buying a Franchise: Insider's Guide to Success* and most people think of what they are doing in those terms, you don't really *buy* a franchise. When you "buy a franchise," you're really buying the *right* to use the company's name and their established way of doing business for a specified period of time. You enter into a franchise agreement with a company and get a license to operate under its name for a specified period of time (typically 5–10 years).

The company's brand name, look and feel, advertising, established procedures, and business methods are the tools you'll use to start and run a successful franchise. At the end of the franchise term, you may renew your contract, under the terms you agree upon with the franchisor. To help eliminate confusion, throughout this book, the phrase "acquire a franchise" is frequently used.

This book is designed to help you clarify your own needs and working style, understand how to evaluate franchises, recognize the key issues in signing and negotiating a franchise contract, and navigate through the thousands of franchise choices out there.

Why a franchise?

You've always wanted to run your own business—be the boss, take charge, set the course. But you don't really want to start a business from scratch. Maybe you don't have that "big" idea or you aren't sure if you have the skills needed to run your own business. You've heard from friends or read in magazines that well-established franchises are a recipe for success—they provide instant name recognition and business processes that are time tested.

Franchise means freedom. Literally. The term comes from an old French word signifying the granting of freedom and rights. And that's what a good franchise gives you: the freedom to operate your own business and the right to hire whomever you want and to make your own business decisions within set guidelines. In the best matches between franchisors and franchisees, franchises reduce the risks inherent in starting a new business and increase your chances for success.

When people think of franchises, companies with instant name recognition and a huge pre-existing customer base such as McDonald's, Merry Maids, 7-Eleven, Gymboree, and Thrifty Car Rental come to mind. These are enormously successful franchises that cost hundreds of thousands of dollars or more to get into. But they are not the only franchises available. Scan publications aimed at entrepreneurs such as *Entrepreneur, Inc.*, and even the *Wall Street Journal* and you'll find a section peppered with ads for other franchise opportunities. There are literally thousands to choose from—everything from pet-sitting companies to document preparation services to tutoring clubs to waste recycling services. Not all of them require huge investments; in fact, some require as little as $5,000 to get started.

The value of a good franchise starts with the value of the brand. As a consumer, if you're going to join a women's workout club, are you more likely to consider a local, stand-alone gym or a nationally known club with established routines and reputation? More often than not, you'll pick the brand name you recognize. The same is true for just about anything you could think of buying, whether it's a meal, a motel room, or a maid service. Consumers want predictable quality, and they get it with franchises.

As a business owner, franchises also give you proven business systems and operations systems. If you were to start a business on your own, you'd need expertise in store design, lease negotiation, business accounting, staffing, merchandising, marketing, financing, advertising, and much more. Most people are good at one or two of those things, but not all of them. A good franchise has the systems and procedures figured out and provides training and ongoing support to ensure your success. Of course, there are still costs and risks associated with acquiring any franchise, no matter how well known the franchise name is.

What a good franchise brings you

The benefits of owning a franchise are numerous, but there is a difference between just *any* franchise and one that is worth your investment. Look for the features that make a franchise a wise investment and beware of warning signs that the franchise is not worth your money.

A worthwhile franchise:

- Produces and markets quality products or services, for which there is a proven demand in your area

- Has established name recognition

INSIDER'S INSIGHT

Bringing Business Dreams to Life

"If the franchised product or service is good, if there is an established value to the trademark, if there is a sound business plan behind the franchised program, and if the franchise agreement has fair protections for both the franchisor and the franchisee, franchising is the answer to all of your business dreams."

Robert L. Purvin,
Chairman and CEO,
American Association of
Franchisees and Dealers (AAFD),
San Diego, California

A Brief History of Franchising

1840s: German brewers give franchises to taverns to sell their ale

1851: Singer Sewing Machine in the U.S. grants franchises to stores as a way to expand sales

Early 1900s: Gas stations and auto dealerships expand rapidly through franchising

1924: Allen & White start A&W Root Beer Drive-Ins

Post World War II: Rapid expansion of franchises in response to growth of suburbs and travel

1950s: Congress passes laws regulating gas and automobile franchises

1955: Ray Kroc opens first McDonald's

1970: Minnie Pearl fried chicken franchise scandal leads to first franchise disclosure laws in California

1978–79: U.S. Federal Trade Commission adopts Uniform Franchise Offering Circular (UFOC) requiring certain disclosures to prospective franchisees

- Has a proven business concept and a successful operating system

- Provides initial and ongoing training

- Offers national and regional marketing and advertising support

- Gives ongoing operational support

- Helps put together your business plan

- Provides or helps find financing for your business

- Helps find the right location and procure a good lease

- Uses part of the royalties paid to the franchisor to provide better support for franchisees and to improve the operational structure of the franchise

- Has a good relationship with most franchisees

- Has a reputation for fairness and support for its franchisees

Beware of any franchise that:

- Can't demonstrate a proven business concept or established operating system

- Does not have a well-established trademark or brand recognition

- Provides minimal or no training

- Supplies little, if any, ongoing support

- Uses the fees franchisees pay primarily for selling more new franchises

- Has a history of conflict and litigation with their franchisees

- Does not provide a list of current or former franchisees

Are Franchises More Successful Than Small-Business Startups?

You will often hear—sometimes from franchise salespeople—that you have a much greater chance at success by acquiring a franchise than by starting a business on your own. Studies differ on whether that is true.

As you would expect, studies touted by the franchise industry tend to show that franchising brings greater success than starting your own business. But other studies, including those done for franchisors, found that franchises succeeded—and failed—at roughly the same rate as independent businesses. Finding a well-run franchise that is a good fit for your goals and skills is the key to success.

The following chart outlines some of the differences between a franchise and an independent business. Remember, the key to success inevitably depends on *you*.

Franchised Business vs. Independent Business

BUSINESS ITEM	FRANCHISED BUSINESS	INDEPENDENT BUSINESS
Concept	Proven concept	Your idea
Franchise fee	Yes	No
Well-known brand name	Yes	No
Training/Support	In worthwhile franchises	You're on your own
Your own vision?	No	Yes
Incur startup costs	Yes	Yes
Pay royalties	Yes	No
Freedom to purchase from any supplier	Not usually	Yes
Pay for advertising	Yes	Yes
Established business practices	Yes	No
Chance of success	Depends on your abilities, finances, market, and strength of the franchise's business plan	Depends on your abilities, finances, market, and strength of your business plan

The Wide, Wide World of Franchises

W hen we think of a franchise, most people think fast food. McDonald's, Subway, Dunkin' Donuts. But every imaginable business has been franchised. There are over 5,000 franchises in more than 85 different business sectors available in the U.S. alone. These range from businesses everybody knows to businesses you may not realize are franchised—senior care, child tutoring, dog grooming, used sporting goods, and party rentals, to name just a few.

And franchises don't only operate out of buildings. As a franchisee, you can conduct business from a mall kiosk that might be selling anything from sunglasses to cell phone covers, from a van providing services from fixing chips in windshields to redecorating your client's home, from a home office doing bookkeeping or children's party planning, and even from an institutional location such as a school or hospital.

The IFA (International Franchise Association) periodically conducts studies on the state of franchising in the U.S. The most recent study, conducted in 2006, gives a snapshot of which franchised business categories are growing fastest and the average costs of starting various franchises.

Some key findings from the study:

- Franchising is booming:
  - 900 new franchise business concepts launched from 2003 to 2006
  - 50% of all retail sales come from franchises
- Largest franchise sectors:
  - Fast food (burger joints, pizzerias, donuts, ice cream)
  - Retail (clothing stores, electronics stores, pet stores, home furnishing stores)
  - Service industries (cleaning services, childcare, oil change services)
- Types of franchises include:
  - Stand-alone store (called standard program)
  - Cart or kiosk (generally located in a mall or other well-trafficked area)
  - Express outlet (generally smaller and with limited products or services)
  - Home office, meaning you can work out of your home
  - Institutional location, such as in a hospital or a school
  - Satellite office that operates as a branch office
  - Mobile or vehicle unit (based out of a motor vehicle)
- Individual franchise fees range from $500 to more than $1 million. The average franchise fee is $25,147. (**Note:** Franchise fees do not cover all startup costs. For more about total costs, see pages 76-88.)

When Is a Business Not a Franchise?

You'll find many businesses advertised in the backs of small-business magazines or online that describe themselves as franchises. Some call themselves "distributorships," "dealerships," or "business opportunities" and state that they are looking for "licensees" or "sales reps." It can be difficult to tell from these ads which are real franchises and which are other types of business opportunities.

If a company is looking for sales reps who will work on salary or on commission, it is not a franchise. A dealership or distributorship may be a franchised business or it may not. There is only *one* clear way to know whether or not the business you are considering is a franchise. All franchised businesses are required by the U.S. Federal Trade Commission (FTC) to give you a specific disclosure document called the Uniform Franchise Offering Circular (UFOC.) (See page 23.) If they don't give you a UFOC, they are not a franchise.

Fast-Growing Franchise Industries

I'm seeing tremendous growth in service businesses—carpet cleaning, oil change, maid services, dry cleaning, senior care, tutoring children, commercial and residential cleaning services, grooming, and taking care of pets. People think of franchises and they think of donuts and hamburgers. But there are lots of other opportunities.

Ellie Vogel, BBB member and founder of Franchise Finder, a franchise consultant firm, Boston, Massachusetts

Partial list of franchise business categories

There is no shortage of business opportunities available through franchising. If you can think of a business, chances are good somebody has franchised it. The following list is just a starting point. Narrow your choices by picking areas you have an interest in or passion for. Picture yourself working in this industry for the next 5, 10, 20 years. If you have existing knowledge or expertise in a particular category, all the better, but it's not required. Remember that within each category, there is a wide variety of options.

ACCOUNTING
Appraiser
Bookkeeping
CPA (Certified Public
    Accountant)
Collection Agency
Debt Counselor
Financial Advisor
Mortgage Broker
Payroll Processor
Tax Preparation

ANIMAL AND PET CARE
Dog Trainer/Dog Walker
Pet Boarding/Kennel
Pet Groomer
Pet Sitter/Animal Daycare
Pet Store Retailer

ART COLLECTING
Appraiser
Gallery Owner

AUTOMOTIVE
Car Wash
Detailer
Gas Station
Muffler
Oil Change Services
Paint
Products and Services
Rental and Leasing
Repair
Stereo
Transmission

BEAUTY/HAIR/ COSMETICS
Bath/Beauty Supplies
Beautician
Color Consultant
Cosmetology/Makeup
    Consultant
Day Spa
Esthetician/Facialist
Hairdresser/Barber
Hairstyle Salon
Image Consultant
Manicurist
Pedicurist
Tanning Salon
Tattoo Parlor/Artist

BOATS

Charters
Repairs
Sales

BUSINESS SERVICES

Adventure Tour Leader
Advertising Specialty Sales
Audiovisual Services for
    Trade Shows
Book Indexer
Bookkeeper
Business Plan Writer
Business Sales Broker
CPA (Certified Public
    Accountant)
Career Counselor
Carpet Cleaning
Caterer
Collection Agency
Courier/Delivery Services
Data Processor
Data Storage Facility
Employee Assistance
Employment Agency
Event/Party Planner
Executive Suite Rentals
Franchise Consultant
Fundraiser
Janitorial Service
Linen Supply Service
Liquidator
Locksmith
Mailing List Service
Management/Business
    Consultant
Market Researcher
Mediator/Arbitrator
Medical Billings and Claims
    Processor
Notary Public
Packaging/Mailing Services
Paralegal
Personal Coach

Plant or Interior Landscape
    Maintenance
Pressure Washing
Print Shop/Printer Supplies
Professional Organizer
Records Processor
Recruiter
Recycler
Relocation Consultant
Signs/Sign Design/Sign
    Painting
Trade Show Consultant
Transcription Services

CHILD- AND FAMILY-RELATED

Adoption Services
After-School Program
Baby Proofing Advisor
Birthday Party Planner
Child Tutor
Childcare Provider
Children's Clothing
College Application
    Consultant
Counselor
Doula/Midwife
Etiquette Advisor
Family Entertainment Center
Magician
Party Rentals
School Bus Service
Sports Coach or Teacher
Toy Retailer

CLEANING SERVICES

Carpet Cleaning
Chimney Sweep
Dry Cleaning
Floors
Graffiti Removal
Laundromat
Maid Services
Window Washing

COMPUTER/ TECHNOLOGY

Animator
Computer Sales/Service
Custom Software Developer
Data Storage
Database Maintenance
Desktop Publishing
Digital Imager
Graphic Artist
IT Specialist
Mailing List Services
Network Installation/Support
PowerPoint Show Designer
Repair/Installation
Search Engine Optimization
Software Consultant
Software Programmer
Solar Energy Equipment/
    Supplies
Technical Consultant
Technical Writer
Trade Show Consultant
Tutor/Training
Website Design/Development
Website Hosting

CONSTRUCTION AND REMODELING

Cabinetmaker
Carpenter
Construction Supply
Electrician
Equipment Rental
Flooring
Furniture Restoration
General Contractor
Handyman
Home or Building Inspections
Homebuilder
Painter
Patio/Deck Builder
Plumber
Remodeling
Retaining Walls
Roofer

EDUCATION

Aerobics Instructor
Art Teacher
Audiovisual Aids Producer
Computer Tutor or Trainer
Dance Teacher
Historical Tour Leader
Language Instructor
Teacher Supply Retailer
Tutor (General)/Private
    Instructor
Tutor (Math)/Private
    Instructor

EMPLOYMENT AND PERSONNEL

Employment Agency
Payroll Processor
Recruiter

FASHION/DESIGN/ CLOTHING

Apparel Designer/Sales Rep/
    Distributor
Apparel Importer
Closet Organizer
Clothing Retailer
Clothing Store
Color Consultant
Embroidery Service
Formal Wear Rentals
Image Consultant
Jewelry Design/Manufacture
Jewelry Repair
Personal Shopper
Second-Hand Clothes Seller
Shoe Designer/Sales Rep
Specialty Medical Apparel

FINANCIAL MANAGEMENT
Appraiser
Collection Agency
Debt Counselor
Financial Planner
Fundraiser
Mortgage Broker
Stock Broker

FOOD
Bakery
Bar Owner
Brewer
Butcher
Cake Maker/Decorator
Caterer
Chef, Personal
Coffee/Tea
Commercial Kitchen Supplier
Convenience Store
Cooking Instructor
Fast Food
Food Safety Consultant
Gift Basket Maker
Health Food Store
Herb Grower/Seller
Ice Cream/Yogurt/Treats
Liquor Store
Organic Farmer
Pizza
Pre-Prepared Meals
Restaurant/Café
Sports Bar
Weight Loss Counselor
Winemaker

GARDENING
Arborist
Gardener
Landscaper
Nursery Owner
Plant/Flower Grower
Pond/Water Garden
   Installation and
   Maintenance
Sod and Sodding Service
Tree/Stump Removal or
   Trimming

HEALTHCARE
Acupuncturist
Adult Day Care
Aerobics Instructor
Dental Hygienist
Driver
Funeral Home Operator
Home Health Care
Hospice Worker
Massage Therapist
Medical/Optical/Dental
   Products or Services
Medical Claims/Billing
Nutritionist/Dietician
Personal Trainer
Senior Care
Speech Therapist
Substance Abuse Counselor
Yoga Instructor

HOME IMPROVEMENT, REPAIR, AND MAINTENANCE
Air Conditioning/Heating
   Repairs
Appliance Repair
Bathtub Refinishing
Chimney Sweep
Closet or Office Organizer
Fence, Patio, Deck Repair or
   Building
Flooring Services
Furniture Cleaning
Garage Door
Gardening
Handyman
Home Stager
Hot Tub Installation/Repair

House Cleaning
House Painter
Interior Decorator
Interior Designer
Pest Control
Plumbing
Pool Installation,
    Maintenance, or Repair
Roofer
Septic Cleaning
Snow Removal
Sod and Sodding Service
Tile Work
Tool Rental
Water Leak Detection
Window Washer

LAW/LAW ENFORCEMENT/ SECURITY

Bail Bondsman
Bodyguard
Collection Agency
Court Reporter
Courtroom Artist
Forensic Artist
Forensic Consultant
Home/Building Inspection
Mediator/Arbitrator
Notary Public
Paralegal
Private Investigator
Private Security
Security Consultant
Security Dog Trainer

MEDIA AND PUBLISHING

Audiovisual Services
Book Publisher
Community Newspaper
    Publisher
Concert Promoter
Desktop Publisher
Freelance Reporter/Writer/
    Editor

Grant Writer
Graphic Designer
Indexer
Marketing/Public Relations
    Consultant
Newsletter Publisher
Résumé Writer
Shopping Mall Event
    Promoter
Trade Show Consultant

PERSONAL SERVICES

Apartment/House Locator
Closet/Personal Organizer
Dating Service
Errand Runner/Personal
    Shopper
Knife/Tool Sharpener
Moving/Hauling
Packing
Relocation Consultant
Résumé Writer
Roommate Matching Service
Taxi

PET-RELATED

Dog Walker
Pet Boarding/Kennel
Pet Cemetery
Pet ID Services
Pet Sitter/Animal Daycare
Pet Store
Pet Supply Retailer

REAL ESTATE

Appraiser
Executive Suite Rentals
Home or Building Inspector
Home Stager
Mortgage Broker
Property Manager
Real Estate Agent
Rental Agency/Locator
Vacation Property Rental
    Manager

RETAIL

Art
Athletic/Sports
Bath/Beauty Supplies
Bookstore
Clothing/Accessories
Electronics
Florist
Gas Station
Gift Store
Hardware
Home Furnishings/
    Home Products
Music
Video Rental

SPORTS, RECREATION/ OUTDOOR

Athletic Trainer
Batting Cages
Bicycle Repair
Event Planner
Golf Driving Range
Historical Tours
Outdoor/Sports Equipment
    Sales
Recreational Therapist
Reunion Organizer
Sporting Goods Distributor/
    Retailer
Sports Coaching/Lessons

TRAVEL/LODGING

Bed & Breakfast Inn
Cruise Agent
Honeymoon Planner
Hotel/Motel Owner
Tour Leader
Tourist Services/Sightseeing
Travel Agent
Vacation Rental Manager

Where Are the Fastest-Growing Opportunities?

According the latest International Franchise Association (IFA) studies, the fastest-growing types of franchises between 2003 and 2006, measured by the number of active brands in that industry then and now, were:

- Retail food: 67% growth. This includes fast food, restaurants, and bakeries.

- Service businesses: 44% growth. These include cleaning services, oil change services, pet care, and child and senior care.

- Real estate: 42% growth. Includes real estate brokers, property management companies, mortgage, home inspection.

- Sports and recreation: 41% growth. Includes youth and sports photography, sporting gear, sports clothing outlets, athletic footwear, nutrition, fitness centers, golf-related businesses, trophies.

- Building and construction: 40% growth. Includes homebuilders, home inspectors, and supplies or equipment sales and rentals.

- Child-related: 38% growth. Includes childcare and tutoring.

- Retail: 33% growth. Includes clothing, furniture, wine, and jewelry stores, florists.

Remember, these statistics measure the number of brands in each business category, not the number of actual franchised units. Franchised units are the physical outlets the company has franchised. (If a particular brand, like Quizno's, has 1,000 franchised units, that's the number of franchised Quizno's restaurants that people can walk into to buy a sandwich.)

From 2003 to 2006, the fastest-growing industries, measured by the increase in the number of actual franchised units were:

- Service businesses: 31%

- Building and construction: 29%

- Child-related: 27%

All three of these experienced growth in excess of 25%.

Next-fastest in growth of number of franchised units were:

- Education-related: 15%

- Maintenance services: 11%

- Real estate: 11%

The Franchise Players

W hether you're going to acquire one franchise or you have larger plans, you'll be hearing about many different kinds of franchise opportunities and players. You already know the basic players: When you acquire a franchise, you become a franchisee. The company from which you acquire the franchise is the franchisor. Other players you may encounter as you explore franchise ownership include:

■ **Single-unit franchisee.** A person who owns one franchised unit. The majority of franchisees are single-unit franchisees, and this is how most franchisees start.

■ **Multi-unit franchisee.** A franchisee who purchases the option to add one or more additional units. The advantage to being a multi-unit franchisee is that it offers the opportunity to make much more money than with a single unit. But there is a downside: If the second or third units fail, not only do you lose the units and the money you invested to start them; you also lose the additional fee you paid for opting for more units.

■ **Area developer/Area director.** An area developer is a franchisee who pays the franchisor for the rights to develop a specific area within a specified amount of time. The larger and more protected the territory (a protected territory is one in which other franchisees

What's in a Concept?

The terms *brand* and *concept* are often used interchangeably, but they have different meanings.

■ The term *brand* refers to the name of a franchise. McDonald's, AAMCO Transmissions, and 7-Eleven are all brands.

■ A *concept* refers to the brand, but it can also refer to a new, distinct franchise program set up by an established company. For example, if a full-service pizza franchise added a take-out-only franchise program, that would be a new concept.

■ The term *category* refers to the general type of franchised business. Healthcare, Automotive, Retail, and Education are all different franchise categories.

■ The term *unit* refers to a single store or operation, whether the business is operated out of an actual store, a vehicle, or a kiosk. If a person owns 3 Merry Maids housecleaning franchises, they own 3 units.

from your franchise can't develop or operate a unit), the more the area developer pays. The option to become an area developer is usually offered by either a young franchise or a more mature one that is expanding into a new area. The advantage of being an area developer is that you have the market to yourself.

The difference between a multi-unit franchisee and an area developer is that the area developer has made *a commitment* to the franchisor to develop a specific number of units within a specific timeframe in a specified area. So if, for example, you're an area developer for a printing shop in northern Washington, you may have agreed to open 5 print shops in northern Washington within 10 years. This will be your territory, and the franchisor won't allow any other franchisees to develop in that area during that time.

■ **Master franchisee.** A franchisee who purchases exclusive rights to develop multiple units in a specific territory. Unlike an area developer, master franchisees develop the territory by selling units to other franchisees. As with the area developer, the benefit of being a master franchisee is that you have the rights to develop units in a specific territory. The downside is that you must make a much bigger investment and take a larger gamble.

The difference between area developers and master franchisees is that, in addition to developing and operating their own units, *master franchisees can also sell franchises* within the territory to other franchisees. So in this case, a person would actually buy a franchise within the specified territory from the master franchisee, rather than from the franchisor. In effect, the master franchisee becomes the franchisor, often providing some of the training and services normally provided by the franchisor and splitting the royalty fees with the franchisor. A person who buys a franchise from a master franchisee, rather than from the franchisor, is called a sub-franchisee.

- **Sub-franchisee.** Someone who buys a franchise unit from a master franchisee, rather than the franchisor. The advantage to doing this is that you're buying a franchise from someone in your region who is familiar with the territory and its needs, as opposed to buying from corporate headquarters, which may be on the other side of the country.

- **Franchise salesperson.** The salesperson works for an individual franchise and is generally the first person you talk to when you contact a franchise for information. In a good franchise, this person is trying to find out whether you are truly a good fit with the company. However, some are simply trying to sell franchises, and if you have the financial means to become a franchisee, they will try to sign you up, whether or not their franchise is the right one for you. Most salespeople will tell you that they are very selective and pick only a small percentage of people who want to become franchisees—and truly successful franchises are highly selective because they don't want stores to fail. It's important to remember, however, that they are salespeople. Their job is to sell you on the franchise, and they won't always have your best interests in mind.

- **Franchise broker.** An individual or company that finds franchises for clients. Brokers do not charge you for their services. They are paid a finder's fee or a percentage of the franchise fee by the franchisor you select. While there are many knowledgeable and capable brokers out there, approach them with caution. Some brokers will steer you only toward those franchisors with whom they work regularly, and this will limit your options. Select a broker who looks at the entire range of franchises available.

■ **Franchise consultant.** A person who is hired by a franchisor to train or audit franchisees or to take on other work, such as marketing and financing. Consultants also help people find franchises. Like brokers, franchise consultants are typically paid by franchisors and don't charge a fee to individuals researching franchises. Check to make sure, however, that the consultant is not steering you only toward the franchisors with whom they regularly work. (See page 69 for more on how to choose a good franchise consultant.)

Is There a UFOC in Your Future?

All franchised businesses are subject to Federal Trade Commission (FTC) rules and regulations that require franchisors to give potential franchisees a specific disclosure document called the Uniform Franchise Offering Circular (UFOC). The UFOC, sometimes referred to as the "disclosure document" or "circular," is the *single most important piece of information* you'll obtain while considering which franchise to acquire. The UFOC is as important to your future in franchising as any of the franchise players you'll meet. That's why an entire chapter of this book is devoted to it (see pages 94-101).

By law, you must receive this document at least 10 business days before you sign a franchise agreement or write a check. It includes all the information you'll need to evaluate before choosing a franchise, including:

- Your obligations as a franchisee

- The franchisor's obligations

- Startup costs

- Royalty and advertising fees

- Termination and renewal terms

- Lists of current and former franchisees of the franchise

- Litigation history of the company

- Information about senior management

If the company is registered with the FTC as a franchise and is required to give you this disclosure document, then it is a true franchise. But remember, the UFOC is a *disclosure* document from the franchisor. It does *not* mean the government has approved the franchise, nor is it a guarantee of any kind. A UFOC from a reputable franchisor will give you an honest overview of costs, responsibilities, obligations, and how the business relationship will unfold. But in *all* cases, you need an experienced franchise attorney to review both the UFOC and the franchise agreement before you sign anything.

Entrepreneur or Intrepreneur?

"*An entrepreneur is someone who could develop their own company. They're independent and like making their own decisions. Franchising takes what I call being an intrepreneur. You run your own business, but you collaborate and align yourself with the direction provided by the franchisor. I ask potential franchisees: Are you going to be able to follow the standards we've put in place? Are you going to be able to follow the programs we provide for you?*"

Jon Jameson, President and CEO,
MaggieMoo's Ice Cream and Treatery,
Columbia, Maryland

Are You *a* Franchise Person?

Who's the Boss?

W hen you join a successful franchise with an established system in place, its structure and name recognition will increase the likelihood that you'll attract and retain customers and succeed in business. But there are some tradeoffs. You'll also give up control over certain aspects of the business.

Even the richest, most powerful franchise owners have to play by the franchise rules. George Steinbrenner, the owner of the New York Yankees, is one of the wealthiest men in the U.S.—and used to getting his own way. But as the owner of a major-league baseball team, which may be the most exclusive franchise system of all, he still has to follow the rules and procedures set by the Baseball Commissioner and other major-league baseball owners.

Having control over all aspects of a business is important to some people and not to others. Knowing what you will and won't have control over can affect which franchise you choose—or whether you choose a franchise at all.

QUICK TIP

Have It Their Way

The amount of operating independence you'll have differs widely among franchises. Some let you run the business your way, but the vast majority require you to run it the "franchise way." Remember: You're purchasing the right and obligation to use a proven system and procedures.

Franchisors control:

- **The territory you serve.** Almost all franchisors define the geographic area your business can serve. This is to guarantee that other franchisees in the same company don't compete for the same customers. Likewise, the franchisor is protecting you by ensuring that others do not encroach on your territory. As a franchisee, you will generally want an exclusive territory to protect your operation, but this will limit your ability to compete in other territories.

- **Where your business site is located.** Many franchisors dictate where new franchise sites can be located, right down to which side of the street your unit may be placed on or how much traffic must pass by your location. This, ideally, is to increase your chances of getting the most customers. The best franchisors will provide demographic data and help you search for a site that will enhance your success.

- **What kind of building you may use.** In some cases, the franchisor owns the land and buildings and leases them back to the franchisee. Reputable franchisors offer fair market prices for rent if they own the property. Others may offer counsel in negotiating the best lease from another property owner.

- **"Trade dress" and design and appearance standards.** Most franchisors require uniformity in appearance, so customers will instantly recognize and feel comfortable with the business. They provided standards and templates for :
  - Logos
  - Signage
  - Store layout, colors
  - Interior furniture
  - Uniforms and other clothing

■ **The goods and services offered**. Franchises restrict the goods and services you can offer. For example, if you acquire a transmission repair franchise, you won't be able to offer brake repair work, even if that's a skill you have. A few franchisors are open to new ideas and allow franchisees to implement new concepts, but this is not the norm.

■ **How you operate.** Franchises use established processes governing everything about how the business runs, including:

- Hours of operation
- Accounting processes and programs
- Bookkeeping methods
- Suppliers
- Financial reporting

■ **Marketing and advertising.** Many franchises require you to spend specific amounts on advertising, in addition to contributing to national advertising campaigns.

Established, big-name franchises are less flexible in their systems. They want things done their way because they've spent years defining and refining their operations. With a successful, established franchise, a large part of what you're buying is the right to use an operating system that works.

Newer, smaller franchises offer more flexibility. They're eager to sign people up in order to grow and are generally willing to bend a little more than mature franchises. If they're just getting started, their systems won't be firmly in place, and they'll allow more experimentation. But excessive flexibility may mean that the franchise doesn't yet have an effective operating system or business plan in place. They may not have yet proven that their business model is successful.

Part of finding the right franchise for you is determining how much freedom of operation you will need to thrive. If operational freedom is important to you, make sure you find out exactly how much freedom you'll have with any franchise you consider. Call the franchisor and ask about their operational procedures, how strictly they must be adhered to, and the consequences of violating them. If you've received a UFOC (see page 23), examine the section that discloses the franchisor's policies and procedures. Then be sure to call other franchisees in the system and ask them about operating hours, sources from which they are allowed to buy supplies, territorial restrictions, design standards, and other aspects of operations that are important to you. If you need a lot of freedom and flexibility in conducting a business, a franchise may not be the right choice for you.

INSIDER'S INSIGHT
Drivers Wanted

Franchisees don't want to reinvent the wheel. They just want to take the wheel that's there for them and drive the heck out of it. If you want to reinvent the wheel, franchising is not where you belong.

Maurice M. Dussaq,
BBB Executive Committee and
Board of Directors member and
owner of two FastSigns franchises,
Reno, Nevada

What Kind of Franchise Person Are You?

Although there is no single "franchise personality," successful franchisees share similar characteristics. One of the most important is that they are driven to get the job done, no matter what it takes. If you own a pizza franchise and one of your employees doesn't show up for a shift, you'll work behind the counter or clean the floors to keep the store running. But that is true of successful independent business owners, as well.

And while franchisees can be entrepreneurial, the successful ones are not so independent that they will be unhappy working inside an established system, controlled by others.

QUICK TIP

'Til Expiration Do Us Part

Signing up to run a franchise is a 5-10 year commitment. Once you've put your name on a franchise agreement, unless you violate the terms or the franchise goes bust, you and the franchisor are in a long-term relationship. A long contract protects you, but it also means you have a long-term commitment. A franchise isn't a business you just try out for awhile.

Characteristics shared by successful franchisees include:

Personal Traits

- **Willingness to work hard.** Running a franchise is not a nine-to-five job. Working long hours and weekends are not unusual, especially in the beginning (and on an ongoing basis, as well).

- **"Fire in the belly."** A burning desire to succeed and a willingness to do what is necessary to make the franchise work.

- **People person.** Whether it's dealing with employees or with customers, successful franchisees get along with people and communicate effectively.

- **A willingness to listen and learn.** No matter how much previous business experience you have, there's always a lot to learn in any franchise because the franchisor wants you to learn and implement *their* system.

- **Ability and willingness to follow a system.** One of the most important things you get when you acquire a franchise is the system. Following it is key. If you like to reinvent the wheel, you'd be better off starting your own business.

Business Skills

- **Sales and marketing.** Most franchisors provide marketing and advertising on a national and regional basis. But you are still responsible for marketing your individual store, which means getting your store's name out into the local community and driving traffic to your location.

- **Business savvy.** Having basic business and accounting skills comes in handy because this means you will have fewer things to learn. Franchisors provide established basic processes, but you still have to do the books correctly and hire appropriate staff.

- **Management.** To grow your business, you'll need to work with many others. If you're in a fast-food franchise, for example, being able to understand and communicate with a teenaged workforce is essential. If you have no experience managing people, you'll need to work to learn the fundamentals of good management practices.

Assess Your Personal Traits

The following worksheet will bring your personality traits into focus and help determine whether running a franchise is a good fit for you.

TRAIT	THAT'S ME	NOT ME
I operate well within established systems, even if I think I have a better way.		
I am a "people person" with good social skills.		
I am a self-starter and a disciplined worker.		
I see things through to the end, even when times are tough.		
I accept that decisions will not always go my way.		
I take instruction and advice from authority figures and experts.		
I know how to ask for help when I need it.		
I will work long hours and weekends when I have to.		
I can learn and follow a new way of doing things.		
I am comfortable leading other people.		
I have good communication skills.		
I can follow a system, but still think "outside the box."		
I am willing and able to thoroughly research a project before jumping in.		
I am motivated to work hard every day.		
I do not expect instant success.		
I can handle emergencies and meet deadlines.		
I'm a leader and can train others.		
I have a high tolerance for risk.		
Total		

Assess the Results

If you checked 15 or more in the "That's Me" column, there's a good chance that you have many of the personal traits needed to become a successful franchisee. Even if a lot of your checks are in the "Not me" column, you can still be successful in a franchise, but you'll need to find a specific kind of franchise.

If you're not a people person, then consider a franchise that allows you to operate individually without a lot of client interaction (such as bookkeeping) or one in which you can hire managers to interact with the public and most employees (such as a tanning salon).

If you are not comfortable working within the systems established by others, you'll need to find a franchise with a great deal of flexibility—or consider starting an independent business instead.

Assess Your Business Skills

Use this worksheet to help determine how well your current business skills will fit with running a franchise operation.

BUSINESS SKILLS	THAT'S ME	NOT ME
I learn new skills and procedures quickly.		
I have the technical expertise or knowledge for the business I am considering.		
I am willing to prepare required financial reports regularly.		
I am comfortable using new technology.		
I have business experience that will help me operate a business.		
I have the ability to sell myself and my products and services.		
I have accounting skills.		
I could run the business myself if I had to lay off personnel.		
I can write a business plan.		
I am good at sales and marketing.		
I am good at networking.		
I have business management experience.		
Total		

Assess the Results

The more checkmarks that appear in the "Yes" column of this worksheet, the stronger a candidate you are for running a successful franchise. A background in business, management, sales, and marketing is definitely an asset. And you'll need to be able to adapt to reporting requirements and procedures of the franchise.

However, if you pick up new skills and procedures quickly, you'll have a good chance at success even if many of your checks were in the "No" column, as long as your franchisor provides substantial training. Look for franchises that have outstanding training programs, not only for their systems and equipment, but also for business fundamentals.

It Takes a Village

E ven if you have chosen the best franchise in the world, the support and help of your family, friends, and loved ones will increase your chances of success. The sooner you get them involved, the better. Starting a new business is a huge undertaking—in terms of both its financial impact and the potential stress on your personal life.

Whether or not family members are working in the business, helping them understand the opportunities, risks, and sacrifices ahead of time is critical. Make sure you and those closest to you are prepared for the reality of franchise ownership. There are a number of issues to consider and discuss, including:

- **Time away from family.** Running a business is a full-time job—and then some. Successful franchisees often put in 60- to 70-hour weeks, especially during the first year. Will your family and friends understand this, or will this time commitment become a cause for resentment? Talk to other franchisees in the system to find out how much time they devote to their businesses.

- **Income fluctuation.** Opening a franchise could mean leaving behind your job and regular paycheck (unless you have a pension or other income source) and living on your savings. Will your savings give you and your family enough to live on after you have paid for your franchise—and until the franchise breaks even? (See Section 4 for more on franchise costs and income.)

Putting the Family to Work

One of the great appeals of franchising is the opportunity it offers you to work with your family. Owning a business can give you the chance to teach your children about business and the benefits of hard work. But this plus can also be a minus. Do you want to be with your spouse or partner 24/7? Some couples can't be together that much without driving each other crazy. Franchisors try to find out how strong a potential franchisee's relationship is if they're planning on working with their spouse or partner. They know that a rocky relationship can put the business at risk.

■ **Impact on retirement benefits.** If you leave a corporate job to open a franchise, you may be giving up future retirement contributions to your 401k or pension fund. Depending on how much you have saved, until your business starts showing a profit, you may not be able to contribute to your retirement accounts.

There are also ways to dip into your 401k or IRA retirement accounts to fund a franchise without tax penalties. But do a thorough analysis of your expenses, savings, and retirement needs before using funds from these sources. Putting your entire nest egg on the line for a business venture is not a good idea.

■ **Stress level.** No franchise is a sure thing. Franchisees in even the most successful systems sometimes fail. You'll no doubt experience increased levels of stress—emotional, mental, and physical—while starting a franchise business. There's pressure to get the business open on time and looking great. And no matter how much work and research you do, you'll inevitably have some fear that the business might fail. That's part of starting a business. There will also be ongoing stress once your franchise is up and running.

■ **Risk to financial security.** Some new franchisees take out loans using the equity on their homes, use all their retirement savings, or max out their credit cards to acquire a franchise—only to have the franchise fail. Avoid this by working with a trusted accountant or financial advisor to determine how much you can afford to invest in a franchise and still have enough to live on, regardless of what happens.

And always have an emergency fund in case of the unexpected. Some years ago, franchisees in the bread and bakery business were thriving. Then the Atkins Diet, with its low-carb emphasis, came on the scene. That meant lean times for the bread and bakery franchisees until the diet's popularity subsided. Franchisees who had enough in savings weathered that storm.

■ **Risk to personal health and health benefits.** Even though you may hire others to do the physical work, you'll sometimes have to do it yourself. That might mean moving a piece of equipment or unloading a shipment of supplies. After a long day at the store, you'll come home at night and do the books. That means less sleep and more stress. Make sure you're in good health and able to wear the many hats a successful franchisee is required to put on.

Before You Commit

"The key is, whatever franchise business you want to do, go in and work as an employee. It takes 30 days of your life. Get in there, roll up your sleeves and learn. Then you'll really know if you like it and want to get into that business."

Chuck Griffin, BBB member and
owner of three Domino's Pizza restaurants,
Santa Cruz, California

Find *the* Right Franchise *for* You

Seventeen Steps to Franchise Ownership

W hat exactly do you have to do to find a franchise? Here are 17 steps to help you narrow your search for the right franchise. These steps will give you a snapshot of the entire process, from your initial search to signing on the dotted line.

In this chapter, you'll get an overview of the franchise-finding process, to help you organize your search for a franchise. You'll learn what franchisors will do and what to expect at each stage.

QUICK TIP

Time Is on Your Side

Slick, 4-color brochures, polished sales pitches, and promises of easy money all conspire to make any opportunity look great, but finding the right franchise takes time. Expect to spend 3 to 6 months researching every aspect of a business—from its financial returns to the viability of the location to how other franchisees like working for the company.

Step 1: Follow your passions

Ask yourself: What's my background? What am I best suited to do? If you're an animal lover and have always wanted to make a living doing something with pets, check out pet-care or pet-grooming franchises. If you have a background in business-to-business sales, consider a print shop or personnel-finding franchise. Make a list of your hobbies, interests, past experience, and education. That will give you a *starting point*. You may find many other franchises that interest you before your hunt is complete, but asking these questions will give you a place to begin.

Step 2: List industries that interest you

Make a list of two or more franchising *industries* you're interested in. (See pages 12-17 for a list of industry categories.) If you already know the industry you want to be in, make a list of several different businesses within that industry. For example, if you know you want to be in the food industry, include several different ones: fast food, restaurant or café, bakery or donut shop, catering, coffee shop, pre-prepared meal companies, and so on. If you're interested in working with autos, list specific types of franchises in that field: gas stations, brake shops, oil change services.

Step 3: Understand the franchise type that's best for you

Make a list of your likes *and* dislikes in terms of the operation of the business and the lifestyle you want. Do you want routine business hours or are you willing to work nights and weekends? How many employees do you want to manage? How do you feel about having a teenaged workforce? Do you want to work with your spouse and be able to hire your kids to work for you?

If you need a nine-to-five schedule, you may eliminate convenience stores and fast-food franchises. If you're not an early riser, that eliminates bakeries and donut shops. This step helps you narrow the field further by figuring out

First Choice?

People often fall in love with a certain franchise concept because they like the product or service or they've had a good experience as a *consumer* of that product or service. But they haven't had the opportunity to learn how the business runs or to understand the implications of being a *provider* of that product or service. It may sound like a lot of fun to have an ice cream franchise, but you could change your mind when you realize you have to work seven nights a week with a mostly teenaged workforce.

As you go through the process of discovering what different franchises expect of you and how that will affect your life (and your family's life), you may change your mind about the particular industry or franchise you want. Take the time to carefully research different franchises and figure out exactly what you can afford and how you'd like your business to fit into your life. Even if you end up with the franchise you first fell in love with, you'll know exactly what you're getting into.

exactly what you want, and equally important, what you don't want.

If you're good at following systems, a more mature franchise will be the best choice because it will have the strictest, proven business practices. If you want more independence, smaller and younger franchises are likely to allow more flexibility.

Step 4: Find franchise listings

Search online for lists of available franchises in your chosen industries. Start with the International Franchise Association, *www.franchise.org*, which promotes the franchise industry as a whole, and the American Association of Franchisees and Dealers, *www.aafd.org*, which looks out for franchisee rights and lists franchisee-friendly companies. Websites such as *www.americasbestfranchises.com*, *www.franchisehelp.com*, and *www.franchisegator.com* are also helpful because they offer franchise directories broken down by business category. Most sites like these only list franchises that pay to be listed with them, so their listings are not complete. Nor do they guarantee that the franchise is a good one. Use several sources when making a list of potential franchises. For a complete list of franchise-finding sources, see Section 8.

Step 5: Get an idea of franchise costs

Once you've started to narrow down the industries and specific franchises that interest you most, you need to get an idea of the costs of those specific opportunities. One way is to go to the websites of the franchises that interest you, to get a bare-bones idea of costs. These will show only the most basic franchise costs; many more expenditures will be associated with starting up. But knowing at least the bare-bones expenses will help you narrow down your choices and get a general idea of how much money you will actually need.

Step 6: Determine your income requirements

How much income do you *need* and *want* from your franchise? Everyone who goes into franchising wants to make lots of money. But what does that mean to you? How much money do you *need* to make? Is the franchise going to be the sole source of financial support for you and your family? Do you have other income? Will the franchise be a part-time operation? Be aware that you may not start making money for quite a while—certainly for more than a year.

What are your long-term financial aspirations? *Put a number on it*. Will $40,000 a year make you happy or do you need to bring in $400,000 a year?

Your income *needs* and *desires* play an important role in the type of franchise you choose. Make certain you are choosing a franchise opportunity that can realistically bring in the money you need.

Keep in mind that franchisors will not give you an exact amount that you can expect to earn because so many variables affect income, even in well-established franchises. Be cautious about franchisors who appear to guarantee you a certain income.

Step 7: Assess your assets

Franchisors want to know what you're worth. Do a thorough assessment of your liquid assets and total net worth. In addition to liquid assets, such as cash and stocks, this includes equity you have in your home or other investments, and 401k, IRA, or retirement accounts that you're allowed to access. Use the services of an accountant you trust to assess your financial situation. Some franchises won't include your home equity or retirement accounts in considering whether or not you can afford their franchise. They don't want you to put all your assets on the line.

Step 8: Contact multiple franchisors

Talk to several franchisors in the industry or industries you're interested in. If there are 10 franchises in a category, pick at least 5 you believe you can afford—and call them. Don't just fall in love with the first franchise you see. You'll have to compare many franchises to have enough information to make an informed decision.

Speak to the franchisor's sales representative and ask for an information packet about the franchise. Ask for all costs and obligations. In addition to information on how the franchise works, the packet will include a form for you to fill out, which provides the franchisor with your financial profile, including your net worth.

Step 9: Fill out franchisor forms

Fill out the initial forms and return them to the franchisors you're serious about pursuing. If you're not willing to provide them with basic financial information about your net worth, they won't take you seriously. If you meet the basic financial requirements, the franchisor will send you their Uniform Franchise Offering Circular (UFOC) (see page 23). Some franchisors send the UFOC immediately after you first contact them, but most want to first see that you have the financial means to acquire one of their franchises and are sincerely interested in doing so.

Step 10: Hire an experienced franchise attorney

It's vital to have an experienced franchise attorney review the company's UFOC. An experienced attorney will provide invaluable advice about the franchising process, operation, and documents. By law, you must have the UFOC for at least 10 business days before you can sign a franchise agreement. Later, you'll need to make sure you and your attorney are comfortable with all aspects of the franchise agreement.

Step 11: Pre-qualify with a lender

Once you know the basic financial requirements for the franchise you'd like to acquire, it's a good idea to pre-qualify for a small business loan before you go further. Doing this makes sense because you'll learn how much you can afford and gain confidence that you can do the deal financially. As with a home, you generally need to put up 20% to 30% of the "down payment," or startup costs, and the bank or lender will finance the rest. Pre-qualifying doesn't commit you to anything; it just makes sure you're ready to sign up when you find the right franchise.

Step 12: Contact current and former franchisees

Current and former franchisees have a wealth of insight into the franchise you're considering. The UFOC lists names and contact information for all current franchisees and franchisees who have left the system within the past year. Ask how they get along (or got along) with the franchisor, how effective the training and ongoing support is (was), and how many hours a week they work (worked). (See pages 122-130 for more on interviewing franchisees.)

Step 13: Talk to potential franchisors

A good franchisor will talk to you for weeks or months to thoroughly explain their system and expectations. Schedule phone appointments with a franchisor over a several-week period so you get to know each other well. These are the people you're going to affiliate yourself with for the next 10 years or more, so make sure they'll be there to support you when you need it. Keep notes on each phone call, including questions asked and the answers given. (See pages 131-141 for more on building a relationship with a franchisor.)

Step 14: Work in a franchise

The only way to really find out whether a particular franchise is a good fit for you is to work in it. Some franchisors, in fact, require that potential franchisees work in the franchise before completing the franchise agreement. Most franchisors have programs that enable you to work in their franchise for a limited time to see if it's a good fit. An opportunity that sounds great on paper may seem a lot different when you actually do the job.

Step 15: Visit the franchisor's corporate headquarters

Meet the senior executives of at least two franchises. To determine whether you're compatible and have common values and goals, it's best to meet the executives face to face. Most franchises have what they call "Discovery Days," where serious candidates fly out to company headquarters to spend an entire day with the senior management team and support staff.

Step 16: Examine the franchise agreement

The franchise agreement is the actual contract you sign when you buy a franchise. A generic franchise agreement is generally sent with the UFOC and is attached as part of Item 22 in the back of the UFOC. It differs from the UFOC because the UFOC is not an actual contract; it is only a document that discloses information. The franchise agreement is a contract you and the franchisor sign, and it becomes legally binding on both parties.

All the information regarding company policy, your rights and responsibilities, and the rights and responsibilities of the franchisor should be the same in the UFOC as in the franchise agreement. But the franchise agreement is not an exact duplicate of the UFOC. Because the UFOC is a disclosure document, it actually contains more information than the franchise agreement. For example, the list of franchisees, the litigation history of the franchise, the business experience of the company officers, and any earnings claims appear in the UFOC, but not in the franchise agreement. If the franchise agreement is not attached to the UFOC, contact the franchisor and ask them to send the agreement to you.

Step 17: Sign the franchise agreement

Federal law states that you must have the UFOC for at least 10 days and the franchise agreement for at least 5 days before signing it. There is a very good reason for this waiting, or "cooling off," period. It gives you a chance to make sure that the verbal promises and claims made to you by company representatives are the same as the claims and promises made in the UFOC and franchise agreement.

Use the time you have to make sure there are no discrepancies between your rights and responsibilities as described in the UFOC and as described in the franchise agreement. *Have an experienced franchise attorney and a trusted accountant review both documents for you.* They'll help you make the right choice. A little money spent up front getting good advice from experienced professionals can potentially save you a lot of money and trouble in the years ahead.

The 5- and 10-day waiting periods are minimum times the law states you must have these documents before signing. But take as long as you need to feel comfortable with the contract before signing. Don't feel pressured to sign before you are ready, whether that's 10 days or 2 months after receiving the contract.

QUICK TIP

Request and Review the UFOC

No matter what else a franchisor sends you, you *must* receive a Uniform Franchise Offering Circular (UFOC) to begin a serious evaluation process. All franchises are required to give you a UFOC, and in all legitimate franchises, the UFOC will reflect what will eventually be in your franchise agreement. If a company won't send you a UFOC, you don't want to deal with them.

What Can You Afford?

To decide whether you can afford to acquire a particular franchise, first estimate the total costs of acquiring and operating it for at least six months, leaving enough working capital in reserve to support yourself and your family. You'll need enough liquid capital (meaning assets that can be easily converted to cash) to pay for at least 20% to 30% of the total initial investment before a lender will consider you. The riskier your franchise, the more collateral the lender will require. This collateral typically includes your home or other property, stocks, bonds, and term deposits.

During your first year of business, you'll need enough working capital to pay your bills and live comfortably while the income from the franchise builds. It's easier if you have a spouse or partner who will provide another source of income. But if you're the sole provider, you'll need either another source of income or enough working capital to live on until your business shows a profit. You don't want to take money from the franchise for your living expenses because that will hurt your franchise's ability to grow and prosper.

If the franchise you like is too costly or will stretch you too thin, consider taking on a partner (see page 160). Always consult with a trusted accountant to confirm your financial limits. If you don't have enough in reserve to operate your business without putting your life savings at risk, then don't acquire that franchise. Look at other franchise opportunities.

Consider the answers to the following questions when you're assessing your ability to pay for a franchise.

- How much of my own money can I afford to invest?
- Will I need outside sources of financing? How much?
- Will I have enough money left over after the startup costs to pay my living expenses until my business turns a profit?
- Do I need or plan to have one or more partners?
- Will I have an additional source of income during the startup phase of the business (part-time job, spouse who works, dipping into 401k, IRA, retirement fund, or other sources)?
- Have I made a complete balance sheet listing all my assets and liabilities?
- How much can I afford to lose?
- Do I have a decent credit rating?

Assess Franchise Opportunities

A ll reputable franchises can succeed. But not everyone can succeed in every reputable franchise. The key to success in franchising is finding a franchise that is not only reputable and honest, but is also the right fit for *you*. That is, it has to fit your goals, financial situation, personality, management style, ability to work with others' rules, and so on. And there must be a known demand for its product or service in *your* market.

The right franchise will also have a proven business concept, which means that the franchisor will have a strong history of successful franchises. If a franchisor has 300 franchises in operation, if there have been very few franchise failures or closures, and if there's low franchisee turnover, that's a sign that they've honed their system well and it works.

What to look for in a franchise

How can you tell if a franchise is a good bet? The best way is to call the current and former franchisees listed in the back of the company's UFOC. Ask them in detail about the way the franchisor works with the franchisees—what kind of training and support they offer, how quickly they respond to questions and concerns, whether they live up to their part of the marketing and advertising bargain, if there are any indications of financial difficulties. (For a list of questions to ask other franchisees, see pages pages 128-130.)

(For a list of questions to ask other franchisees, see pages pages 128-130.)

INSIDER'S INSIGHT

Under the Microscope

" *With most good franchises, they're evaluating you as much as you're evaluating them. And if they're not, you don't want to be with them. All they're trying to do is sell the franchise. They aren't really concerned with your long-term success.* "

Maurice M. Dussaq,
BBB Executive Committee and
Board of Directors member and
owner of two FastSigns franchises,
Reno, Nevada

Key concerns include:

- **Franchise support for franchisees.** Almost all franchisors require you to pay royalties. In the case of worthwhile franchises, a lot of that money is plowed back into improving the operational structure of the franchise and providing better support for franchisees. In other situations, the money goes into simply trying to sell more franchises. How can you tell which approach a franchisor will take? The best way is to call and talk to a lot of franchisees within that franchise. But you can also tell by looking at the UFOC to see how big the company's support staff is and what their job responsibilities are. If a company has 300 franchisees and only 15 people on staff, and most are devoted to sales, you're not going to receive much support. But if it has 70 staff members dedicated to supporting those franchisees, you have a much better chance of getting the support you need.

  Also note how careful the franchisor is in evaluating your suitability to be a franchisee. In the best franchises, the franchisor wants to make sure there's going to be a good long-term fit between you and the franchise. If they're too eager to take your franchise fee without asking you a lot of tough questions and if they're only painting a rose-colored picture of how easily you'll make big money, they may not be a good fit for you, no matter how much you love the business they're in.

- **Franchisee associations.** A reputable franchise allows its members to form franchisee associations. These are groups of franchisees who meet and take common concerns to their franchisor. The greater the number of franchisees involved, the more seriously the franchisor will take those concerns. Historically, franchisors have been resistant to such associations. They haven't wanted a small group of dissident franchisees telling them what to do. However, associations are now more and more accepted by franchisors.

A good franchisee association can provide an effective channel of communication between the franchisor and franchisees. It can provide useful information from the field that can change the way the franchise operates. It gives the franchisees a voice and an effective way to make sure that voice is heard. A franchisor that doesn't permit its franchisees to form associations is more likely to have angry, resentful franchisees who have no effective way to change bad franchisor policies. The American Association of Franchisees and Dealers (*www.aafd. com*) keeps an ongoing list of association-friendly franchisors on its website.

■ **Company-operated locations.** Most franchises have both company-run stores (stores owned and operated by the corporate parent) and stores run by franchisees. A good franchise has a high percentage of franchised outlets compared to company-run stores. That means they have a lot of experience training and supporting franchisees. A company with just a small number of franchised outlets will not have the infrastructure to support you well. How can you tell? Information about the number of franchised outlets and company-owned stores is in the UFOC.

QUICK TIP

Frequent Flyer Miles

Unless you happen to live in the same community as the franchise you choose, you'll travel to their headquarters for training. Most franchisors do not pay for travel to and from the location or for hotel and meals. One way to save money is to use frequent flyer miles for the flights and hotel points for the accommodations. And stay in a hotel room with a small kitchen so you're not eating out for every meal.

Training

The initial training provided by a well-run franchisor is typically one to two weeks long. In most companies, experts from the franchise run these sessions. You'll travel to the company's headquarters and get a combination of classroom and hands-on training.

These are long days—often between 10 to 14 hours—but the training is well worth it. You'll be introduced to what you need to know to run that franchise—both the actual operations of the business itself and the administrative and financial details. In one franchise, the first day focuses on accounting, how to set up and maintain profit & loss statements, and how to use QuickBooks or other accounting programs. The second day covers sales and marketing. Another day focuses on preparing financial and other weekly, monthly, and quarterly reports the franchise requires, as well as how to use point-of-sale systems and methods of managing inventory. There's also a day devoted to administrative and staffing issues.

Depending on what type of franchise you are involved with, at least one day may be devoted to the technical aspects of that franchise. If you're going into the trophy business, there will be a course on engraving. If you're going into the quick-print business, you'll be trained in the latest relevant software and hardware.

After time in the classroom, the next step in training is actually working in a franchise. Whether it's a pet-grooming service or a fast-food franchise, you'll spend time—anywhere from a few days to a couple of weeks—working there. You'll get hands-on experience in every aspect of the business, including interacting with customers, operating the cash register, and preparing the product or providing the service.

After the initial training, you'll get follow-up support for the grand opening of your franchise. The best franchisors send a representative to your location to help you get organized and open your store. This covers everything from how to put up shelving to the best way to use the various wall, counter, and floor displays. If appropriate, they'll also make sales calls with you to teach the most effective methods for conducting and closing the calls.

If you're in a good franchise, at the end of training you'll feel as if you can hit the ground running. You'll feel confident that the people you've met from the franchise will be there for you when you have more questions or run into problems. Not that they'll solve every problem for you, but if you get stuck when trying to deal with issues that come up, they'll help guide you to the solution. Reputable franchisors want you to have the knowledge to be successful. In the long run, if you're successful, they're successful.

Advertising and marketing

One of the benefits you seek when choosing to acquire a franchise is the ability to ride the coattails of a well-known brand name and national advertising. Franchises vary as to the degree of marketing and advertising support they provide. Only the largest offer major national ad campaigns. Most franchises charge at least a 2 percent fee, based on gross revenues, for general advertising and marketing support. That's in addition to your franchise royalty payments. A reputable franchise's fees are clearly stated in the UFOC and franchise agreement.

QUICK TIP

Local Motion

Well-established franchisors provide national and regional ad campaigns. But *you* are generally responsible for creating and paying for the local advertising that will drive customers to *your* outlet. Ask the franchisor exactly what marketing and advertising they pay for and remember to include your own advertising costs in your business plan.

Franchises have a multi-tiered system, where the money goes into three different "buckets": one for national, one for regional, and one for local advertising. Local money is often earmarked to promote the overall brand, not to advertise *your* particular franchise. And smaller and newer franchises generally have only two buckets: regional and local.

Most medium and large franchisors have a marketing department. They conduct demographic studies to be sure their franchise will be successful in a given area, devise marketing strategies and ad campaigns, and test them for effectiveness. They'll create and produce displays, banners, coupons (like "buy one, get one free"), flyers, and inserts that you can personalize by adding your outlet's address and hours.

In addition, a group of franchisees in a specific region may work together and use funds from the regional marketing budget to buy ads covering your region. Some franchisors require a separate payment for regional advertising because the main advertising fee covers only national efforts. Even though this is an extra expense, it's more affordable than buying ads yourself because a group can get better rates, as it is buying more ad space than an individual operation.

Local marketing is an expenditure of time, as well as money. If you're doing your own local marketing, most franchises require pre-approval of any materials that use their logo and trademark. When you contribute to local charitable events to increase awareness of your outlet's name in the community, that effort comes from you, not the franchisor. Even with a known national brand, your involvement in the local community will benefit your franchise.

How can you tell if a franchisor provides adequate advertising and marketing? Some provide a lot and some provide none. Those that do provide advertising and marketing usually charge about 2% of your gross sales for these services. The best way to find out if these efforts are effective is to call several other franchisees in your region. Ask them what they think of the company's advertising and marketing efforts. Are they effective in driving enough customers to the store or point of service to be successful? And ask them what they think the company could be doing better.

Red flags and warning signs

If a franchise is either not mature enough or does not have enough expertise to be successful (or is fraudulent), there will be warning signs. These signs do not always mean you should avoid a franchise, but if you discover any of them, do extra research to understand exactly what you're getting—or not getting—with the franchise. You can uncover this information by carefully reviewing the UFOC and the franchise agreement—and speaking with other franchisees. Red flags to watch for:

- High number of franchise failures or rapid turnover of franchise outlets. If more than 5%–10% of the franchises have failed or changed hands over a three-year period, you should investigate the reasons for the failures or turnovers very carefully.

- Lots of litigation against the franchise or many complaints filed. It's not uncommon for a company to have one or two lawsuits brought against it. But more than that is cause for concern. Investigate the nature of the litigation and how it was resolved.

- Pressure from the franchisor to sign an agreement before they give you adequate time to let you and your attorney review it. You and your attorney should have as much time as you need to review the agreement. The law states that you must have the UFOC for at least 10 days and the franchise agreement for at least 5 days before signing. But don't rush this process! Take as much time as you need to familiarize yourself with and get completely comfortable with the terms of the agreement. If you need one or two months, that should not be an issue.

- Too few franchisees from the company to talk to. If you are given only two or three names of franchisees, you won't get enough information to make an informed decision.

- A brand-new or very young franchise with no history of success.

- Franchisor who is quick to accept you without making sure you're financially qualified and well suited to succeed. This could mean the franchise is trying to grow by signing up anyone who can come up with the franchise fee.

- A history of bankruptcy or numerous company name changes.

- Lack of a rigorous training program.

- No registered trademark or trademark pending for the company.

- If more than 10%–15% of franchisees have major complaints about the franchisor, investigate carefully why this is so. There may be bad chemistry between the franchisor and these franchisees or the franchisor may provide very poor support.

- Too much flexibility in the franchise system. This could mean either that the franchisor doesn't have a proven business model yet or that they're more interested in selling the franchise than ensuring its success.

QUICK TIP

Company-Owned

Most franchises have both company-run outlets and outlets run by franchisees. A company-run outlet is owned and operated by the corporate parent. Look for franchises that have a high percentage of franchised outlets compared to company-run outlets. That means they have a lot of experience training and supporting franchisees.

Recognizing Worthwhile Franchise Opportunities

A WORTHWHILE FRANCHISE	DON'T INVEST IF
Has a proven business concept and a successful operating system.	There's no proven business concept or operating system. If the franchise is new and untested, it won't have a track record of success. Generally, wait to invest until a franchise system has been in operation for at least 18 months.
Provides comprehensive training: usually 1–2 weeks of intensive, on-site learning and additional, ongoing training.	Minimal or no training offered.
Supplies marketing support (brochures and posters).	Minimal, if any, marketing support offered.
Has name recognition and a reputation for quality in your area.	The company's name has little or no brand recognition or name value.
A significant portion of royalties paid to the franchisor go into providing increased support for franchisees and operational improvements.	The royalties paid to the franchisor are primarily used to market and sell new franchises.
Runs ongoing effective advertising campaigns.	Leaves you responsible for most or all advertising.
Allows franchisee organizations and associations that have negotiating leverage with the franchisor.	The franchisor does not permit its franchisees to form franchisee associations.
Has a good relationship with most franchisees—including good communication and ongoing operational and marketing support.	The franchisor has a record of conflict and a history of litigation with franchisees.
Uses franchised outlets as its main mechanism for product or service distribution. Has only a small percentage of company-owned units. This means they have a lot of experience in training and supporting franchisees.	The franchisor has a large percentage of company-owned outlets, as opposed to franchised ones.
Has an established and accepted trademark for its business, which means you don't have to spend time and energy building a recognizable brand.	The franchise doesn't have a well-established trademark or has no trademark registered.
All promises and obligations stated verbally and in the company's disclosure document (UFOC) are in the final franchise agreement.	Promises made verbally or in the UFOC are not in the final franchise agreement.
Provides you with the names of all current franchisees and those who have left the system in the past few years.	The franchisor does not provide a list of current or former franchisees or is reluctant to do so.

Continued

Recognizing Worthwhile Franchise Opportunities

A WORTHWHILE FRANCHISE	DON'T INVEST IF
Produces and markets quality products or services for which there is a proven market demand in your area.	No proven demand for the franchise's products or services in your area.
Provides assistance putting together the business plan, including financing or helping you get a loan from a reputable lender.	You're on your own when preparing the business plan and finding financing.
Offers guidance in finding the right location and in procuring a good lease.	You're on your own when seeking a location and a lease.
Has a reputation for fairness and support for its franchisees.	Franchisor has an adversarial relationship with many of its franchisees. Many franchisees are disgruntled by lack of support. It's not uncommon for one or two franchisees to be unhappy. But if more than 20% of the total number of franchisees have major complaints, consider other franchise opportunities.
Evaluates your suitability carefully before offering you a franchise.	Franchisor does not spend time evaluating whether you're a good fit for the business, but simply offers you the franchise if you pay the franchise fee.
Encourages you to work in a franchise within its system before deciding to become a franchisee.	The franchisor offers no program to allow you to work in their system before becoming a franchisee.

Where to Search for Franchise Opportunities

Many organizations, websites, books, magazines, and conferences exist to help you research and acquire a franchise. Some of the most useful are included here. Websites are constantly changing and evolving, so check them often for the most current information.

Websites

Many websites are devoted to franchising. New ones crop up from time to time, and changes are made to existing ones frequently. Among the most trafficked sites:

- *www.americasbestfranchises.com* offers a franchise directory and resources to help you find financing for your franchise. Franchise directory listings are presented by franchisors, but the website also has links to FranSurvey, which interviews franchisees from various franchises, in order to rate franchisors.

- *www.business.gov* is a U.S. government website that provides good general information about acquiring a franchise.

- *www.franchisehandbook.com* or *www.franchise1.com* produces the quarterly *Franchise Handbook*, a directory of 1,700 franchises in 65 categories. It also has an online database of franchises, franchise consultants, and franchise conferences.

- *www.franchisehelp.com* has a franchise directory and fee-based research and reports, including industry surveys and reports on various franchise sectors and companies. UFOCs are available for purchase, and there are special sections for potential franchisees, including help with franchise selection.

- *www.franchisegator.com* has a franchise directory with frequent updates on available franchises, feature articles on financing, and listings of upcoming franchise conferences. The directory presents franchisors' descriptions but does not critically compare various franchises.

- *www.franchisesolutions.com* has a franchise directory, news and advice columns, and special sections for women and veterans. The articles tend to be industry fluff pieces.

- *www.franmarket.com* has information on financing, startup strategies, marketing, and other issues for franchisees, as well as a directory of franchises available worldwide. The website is produced in conjunction with SCORE, the Service Corps of Retired Executives.

- *www.nase.com* is the National Association for the Self-Employed and calls itself "The Nation's Leading Resource for Micro Businesses." It provides a lot of information on starting and running a business and offers group health insurance, a great benefit for franchisees.

- *www.startupjournal.com* is published online by the *Wall Street Journal* and is aimed at budding entrepreneurs. It has a section devoted to franchising and a section listing franchises for sale. Articles include "Franchisee Knows Value of Good Employees" and "First-Time Franchisees Face Tougher Road."

■ *www.worldfranchising.com* lists Bond's 100 Top Franchises and Bond's 50 Under 50 Franchises—50 up-and-coming franchises with under 50 units. The site also includes links to its sister websites to help you find a franchise attorney or franchise consultant. Included on this site is a section listing franchisors dedicated to increasing representation by members of minority communities.

Print directories

Print directories of franchises offer a wealth of information. Some are updated quarterly, but most have annual updates. Check directory websites to order the most current version. The following are among the most useful directories.

■ **Bond's Franchise Guide.** An annual guide with detailed profiles of over 1,000 franchisors in 45 business categories. Cost: $29.95. Available from *www.sourcebookpublications.com* or from *www.worldfranchising.com,* at the Franchise Bookstore.

■ **Bond's Top 100 Franchises.** An annual list of top franchises in the food-service, retail, and service-based industries. Companies are evaluated on many factors, including franchisee satisfaction, level of initial training and ongoing support, market dynamics, and financial stability. Cost: $19.95. Available from *www.sourcebookpublications.com* or from *www.worldfranchising.com* at the Franchise Bookstore.

■ **The Franchise Handbook.** A directory of 1,700 franchises in 65 categories, updated quarterly. Each listing has a description of the franchise, address, contact and phone number, as well as franchise fee, total initial capital investment, number of franchises, type of training offered, and other information. Cost: $6.99 per issue or $22.95 for 4 issues. Available at *www.franchisehandbook.com.*

- *The Franchise Opportunities Guide.* Published by the International Franchise Association twice a year. This franchise directory offers brief company description, initial investment required, training provided, and contact information. Cost: $17.00. Call 1-800-543-1038 or go to *www.franchise.org* for more information.

- *Franchise Times' Super Book of Franchise Opportunities.* This large franchise directory offers complete descriptions, contact information, and investment profiles. It will be updated regularly on the Franchise Times website. Available at *www.franchisetimes.com.*

- *Franchise Update Publications.* This company offers several guides, including *The Executive's Guide to Franchise Opportunities*, *Food Service Guide to Franchise Opportunities*, and *The Guide to Multiple-Unit Franchise Opportunities*. Available at *www.franchise-update.com.*

- *How Much Can I Make?* This book details the earnings claims of 112 different franchise operations. The information is provided by the franchisors through their Earnings Claims Statements. This data provides a starting point only for helping you figure out how much you might make in a similar business. Cost: $29.95. Available from *www.sourcebookpublications.com* or from *www.worldfranchising.com,* at the Franchise Bookstore.

QUICK TIP

Business Opportunities vs. Franchises

Franchises advertised in the backs of magazines or online are usually described as franchises but some are called distributorships, dealerships, or business opportunities. These may or may not be franchises. The only way to know whether or not the business you're considering is a franchise is to ask for a copy of their UFOC. If they don't have a UFOC, they're not a franchise.

■ ***Minority Franchise Guide.*** This directory has profiles of almost 500 companies that encourage and support minority franchisees. Cost: $19.95. Available from *www. sourcebookpublications.com* or from *www.worldfranchising. com*, at the Franchise Bookstore.

Trade shows, conferences, and seminars

Trade shows are a great way to be introduced to multiple franchises in a short amount of time. Numerous conferences and trade shows are held coast to coast year round. These shows include educational forums that give you the opportunity to meet representatives of many franchises in person. Some shows combine franchises with other business opportunities.

Franchisors hand out promotional brochures at these events, and some also hold mini-seminars on their franchise and even give out their UFOC to people they consider serious candidates. To be considered a serious candidate, you have to fill out a financial profile to pre-qualify. You can find current conference schedules on most of the websites listed on pages 66 and 67.

You can't actually buy a franchise at a trade show. Even if a franchisor gives you the UFOC, there is a legally required 10-day "cooling off" period between the time when you receive the UFOC and the point at which you sign a franchise agreement. So if a company says they can sign you up that day at a trade show, it's not a franchise.

The U.S. Small Business Administration (SBA) sponsors seminars in many communities through Small Business Development Centers (SBDCs). Search on the Internet for SBDCs in your community, which are often located on college campuses. Taught by college professors, these seminars sometimes include information about starting a franchise.

Some of the bigger trade shows and conferences include:

- **AAFD Annual Conference.** The conference of the American Association of Franchisees and Dealers (AAFD) focuses on building fair franchising standards and improving franchisee associations but also has franchise exhibitors, networking opportunities with other franchisees and suppliers, and free consultations with business experts. It's more for existing franchisees but could also be useful if you're on the verge of acquiring a franchise. Cost: $375–$425. Go to *www.aafd.org* for more information.

- **Franchise and Business Opportunity Conferences.** This traveling show takes place almost every month in various cities throughout the U.S. and Canada. It brings buyers and sellers together, providing opportunities to meet franchisors (or their sales reps) in person to find out more about various franchises. Seminars are also offered on topics such as financing a franchise or leasing. Admission is generally $10. For information, call 1-800-891-4859 or go to *www.franchiseshowinfo.com*.

- **Franchise Expo South.** This show serves the southeastern U.S., Latin America, and the Caribbean. Along with a conference program, the three-day event brings franchisors together with potential franchisees. Basic admission is $15 per day, and there are extra fees for some symposiums. Go to *www.franchiseexposouth.com* for more information.

- **IFA Annual Convention.** The International Franchise Association's annual convention is a massive, four-day event with general and break-out sessions covering everything from effective communication between franchisors and franchisees to effective marketing techniques. This convention is geared more toward franchisors than franchisees, but there's plenty for franchisees, as well. There are keynotes by industry luminaries, an exhibitor hall, and lots of networking opportunities.

Admission, including conference and seminars, is $899. Go to *www.franchise.org* for more information.

- **International Franchise Expo.** Sponsored by the International Franchise Association, this annual event showcases hundreds of franchise concepts, attracting franchisors, investors, and potential franchisees from throughout the U.S. and 80 other countries. The three-day event also has a conference program. For more information, go to *www.franchiseexpo.com*.

- **Multiunit Franchising Development Conference & Expo.** Organized by Franchise Update, this conference is for franchisees interested in becoming multi-unit operators and brings together franchisors, franchisees, suppliers, and investors. Go to *www.areadeveloper.us/mudco/* or *www.franchise-update.com* for more information.

- **West Coast Franchise Expo.** This is an annual, three-day event sponsored by the International Franchise Association, aimed at potential franchisees from over a dozen states in the West. It showcases over two hundred franchise concepts, representing a wide variety of industries at all investment levels. In addition to the exposition, a full conference program and numerous seminars are offered. Go to *www.wcfexpo.com* for more information.

A variety of other franchise trade shows takes place across the U.S. Some of these are sponsored by a single franchisor with multiple brands. For example, Raving Brands (*www.ravingbrands.com*) is a company with nine different franchise brands under one corporate umbrella. It takes its "tour days" to various cities across the country to sell franchises and usually meets in airport hotels. These types of shows can be helpful for gathering information about particular brands, but they are limited to the offerings of the one parent company.

Magazines

Several magazines regularly cover the franchise industry, and they're full of advertisements for franchising opportunities. Look in the backs of the magazines for the ads.

- **Entrepreneur.** Monthly magazine for the small business-person. Covers franchising consistently. The magazine rates franchises and has an annual "Franchise 500," the 500 top franchises selected by the editors of the magazine. Subscription is $16 per year through *www.entrepreneur.com* or call 1-800-274-6229. Single issues also available on newsstands.

- **Franchise Market Magazine.** Published quarterly in cooperation with SCORE (Service Corps of Retired Executives) and distributed in 389 SCORE offices nationwide. Also available online at the website. It has features like "10 Dumb Things to Avoid When Buying a Business." It also includes the Top 100 New Franchises started since 2000. Go to *www.franmarket.com* for more information.

- **Franchise Times.** News and features covering the franchise industry, aimed at franchisees and franchisors alike. Lots of information available on franchise financing and opportunities to acquire a franchise. Subscription is $35 per year. Call 1-800-528-3296 or go to *www.franchisetimes.com.*

- **Franchise Update.** Geared more toward franchisors than franchisees, this quarterly magazine has listings of franchises for sale. Subscription is $40 per year. Go to *www.franchise-update.com* for more information.

- **Franchising World.** Published monthly. The official magazine of the International Franchise Association (IFA). Subscription is $50 per year. Call 1-800-543-1038 or visit *www.franchise.org.*

■ *Inc.* Magazine aimed at the small business entrepreneur. Its website has a franchise directory. Special features and how-to guides on acquiring a franchise, financing, raising capital, and finding a mentor. Online subscription rate is $10 per year. Go to *www.inc.com* for more information. Single issues also available on newsstands.

Should You Use a Franchise Consultant?

A franchise consultant is a person or firm that helps find you a franchise. They'll do everything from determining your suitability from both a financial and a personal perspective to conducting assessments to find out what types of franchises fit well with your skills and personality type. If you're not a good franchisee candidate, they'll tell you.

Franchise consultants are typically paid by the franchisor once you sign the franchise agreement. You pay nothing, but there is a downside to this "free" service: Consultants work with franchisors they know and like and steer you toward those franchisors, which limits your options. You can also hire an independent consultant and pay a fee to help you find a good franchise. But be prepared to do some of the legwork yourself. Unless you also research franchisors on your own, you won't necessarily find the best opportunities for you.

There are more than 700 franchise consultants in the U.S. How do you choose a good one? Make sure that the consultant you're considering working with is independent and can work with any and all franchisors. Check to see if the consultant is a member of the Better Business Bureau or if the BBB has a Reliability Report on the consultant.

You can search for franchise consultants by entering the term *franchise consultant* and the city you live in into any search engine. You can also start your search on these websites:

■ *www.bbb.org.* Look under "Check Out a Business" to find a BBB Reliability Report

■ *www.aafd.org.* Look for resources under "Buying a Franchise" to find a consultant.

■ *www.franchise.org.* Look under "Finding the Right Franchise for You."

Acquiring an existing franchise

Sometimes you can acquire a franchise that is already up and running, rather than having to start from scratch. You can acquire an established business from an existing franchisee or acquire a company-owned outlet that the franchisor wants to convert to a franchise. Franchises may be sold or converted for several reasons. Sometimes the current franchisee wants to retire or change careers. In other instances, a franchisor may decide to convert a company-owned outlet to a franchise because they've had a hard time managing the operation from company headquarters and believe a local franchisee would do a better job. A franchise may also be for sale because it is simply in a bad location. Investigate buying an existing franchise as carefully as you would a brand-new franchise.

When you acquire an existing franchise, you'll still have to be approved by the franchisor and go through the training program. However, the sale price will be negotiated between you and the existing franchisee.

You can contact franchises directly to find franchises for sale or you can search online through the Business Resale Network (*www.br-network.com*), which lists both existing franchised and non-franchised businesses for sale.

Get complete financial information on the existing business and its history of profit and loss. Do this by requesting tax statements, as well as profit-and-loss and cash-flow statements from the past three years. Find out why the owner is selling. Did the owner simply want to retire or is the store in a bad location? Is there little demand for the product or service in that area? Has the store been poorly run? Don't assume you'll have more success than the last owner, because there may be other reasons behind the poor performance.

There are advantages and disadvantages to acquiring an existing franchise, including:

Advantages

- **Proven track record.** You're not guessing about the store's performance potential or looking at estimated earnings. You'll see actual financial statements from that store and know what the profit and loss and cash flow have been.

- **Faster financing.** The existence of real financial records makes it easier to get financing quickly (assuming it's a profitable business).

- **Established customer base.** The business has an established reputation in the community and an existing base of customers.

- **Existing location.** The location, lease, and build-out are complete.

- **Equipment installed.** The special equipment needed to operate is acquired and operational.

- **Trained staff.** A trained staff is in place, so you don't have to find and train new employees before you open your doors.

- **Immediate revenue.** You'll be in business right away, instead of having to wait the months it takes to get a new franchise up and running.

Disadvantages

- **The outlet may be in a bad location.** There may not be much traffic, or perhaps the outlet has a high sales volume but is located in a high-crime area.

- **Declining demand.** Demand for the product or service in your area may be declining for whatever reason, and that could be why the current franchisee wants out of the business.

- **Bad lease.** The lease could be bad, which could mean anything from the fact that it will expire shortly to the rent being about to go up substantially.

- **Underperforming outlet.** The outlet may not have a good track record and the franchisor may frequently find new franchisees to operate it.

- **Requires improvements soon.** It could be an old franchise that needs substantial new investment to upgrade equipment or décor.

- **Transfer fees.** You'll have to pay a transfer fee and legal costs for the sale.

- **Not a full-term contract.** You don't always get a full 5- to 10-year term contract from the franchisor.

QUICK TIP

For the Records

If an existing franchisee selling their store is unable to document their financial claims, don't acquire the franchise. Sometimes people claim they are running a cash business and their records don't show money taken "under the table." If you can't document the difference between what the owner claims the business makes and what the records actually show, move on.

Franchise Pretenders

Not every business opportunity claiming to be a franchise actually is one. To be certain that any business you're interested in is a legitimate franchise, make sure that they can provide a UFOC. Any business that can't provide one is not a franchise.

Other ways to spot pretenders:

- The company puts out promotional materials or sales pitches claiming you'll make big money fast, regardless of your lack of experience or training.

- The business opportunity is offered for only a short time.

- The deal is promoted as a sure thing, with guaranteed security for years to come.

- The company claims you'll reap large financial rewards from working part time or not at all.

- The company asks for money up front. A legitimate franchise will not want money in advance and can't ask you to sign a franchise agreement until you've had the UFOC for 10 business days.

- The company does not sell their product or service where they are headquartered. People running a scam often won't take the chance of selling in their own area.

- The company has not been in business long. Find out how long the company has been in business and verify with a third party. Complaints and problems with companies sometimes don't surface for a year or two. The longer a company has been in business, the easier it is to verify its legitimacy.

- The company charges a high fee for a lesser-known franchise. This could indicate that the company is interested mostly in selling the franchise and not in providing the support needed for the franchisee to succeed after the sale.

- Your income as franchisee is based primarily on recruiting other distributors or dealers, rather than selling products or services directly to consumers. These are multi-level marketing (MLM) or networking programs, not franchises.

- You don't have exclusive territory.

Show Me the Money!

"One of the biggest mistakes I see new franchisees make is underestimating the amount of capital they need to get their franchise going."

Maurice Dussaq, BBB Executive Committee
and Board of Directors member and
owner of two FastSigns franchises,
Reno, Nevada

How Much Will *it* Cost?

Cost Overview

M any of the costs of starting a franchise are the same as those associated with starting any new business. But some costs are unique to franchises. In particular, franchise fees and royalties are fees you'll encounter with virtually every franchise.

Ideally, some of these costs may actually save you money. For instance, you might spend a lot of time and money perfecting your product or service, while a worthwhile franchise already has a proven product or service. You pay an initial franchise fee for this, but it might be less than you would have spent figuring out what to sell. You'll also pay ongoing royalties to the franchisor, but if they have a reliable system for running a business, those royalties may be less than the cost of systems you would have had to devise on your own.

However, franchise costs are likely to be far more fixed than those in an independent business. You may also have to pay these fees whether or not you are profitable. So it's important to understand the whole range of fees and expenses you'll encounter as a franchisee.

QUICK TIP

A Seat at the Table

A franchise fee is the initial payment you'll make to use the franchise brand name and business systems. It does not cover startup and operational costs, which can be several times the franchise fee. Expect your initial cash outlay to be 5 to 10 times more than the franchise fee.

QUICK TIP

A License to Sell

When totaling up all your startup expenses, keep in mind that a franchisor does not supply any of the licenses or permits you'll need to do business. You'll have to apply and pay for all the necessary business licenses and permits required to operate in your city and state.

Franchise fees

The franchise fee is the amount charged by a franchisor to grant you a license to do business under their name. It is a one-time, up-front fee paid to the franchisor when you sign the contract. Paying a franchise fee gives you the right to use a company's name and operating system.

When you're investigating various franchises, the franchise fee is one of the first things you'll want to learn about. The amount of the franchise fee is usually listed on the home page of the franchise's website. If it's not there, call the franchisor's home office and ask to speak to a salesperson who can tell you what the franchise fee is.

The franchise fee is normally due and payable at the time you sign your franchise agreement. However, some companies let you pay a portion of the fee (usually half to two-thirds) when you sign the franchise agreement and the remainder sometime prior to the grand opening. Others let you pay the franchise fee in two or three equal installments. Franchise fees are not generally refundable, but some companies will refund your franchise fee within the first 30 days if you decide to back out of the deal.

Franchise fees vary widely—from as low as $500 to as high as $1 million. But very few franchises are at either the high or the low end of those extremes. The average franchise fee is about $25,000. Franchise fees also vary a lot from one company to the next within the same industry. For example, one bakery franchise has a $15,000 franchise fee, while another has a fee of $35,000.

A lower fee is not automatically a better deal, nor does a higher one necessarily guarantee better services. A lower fee may mean the franchise makes it easier for people to get in, but the franchisor offers very little support and has no name recognition or proven business model. A higher fee may mean the company makes most of its money from the franchise fee and offers very little ongoing support. The franchise fee must be judged in the context of the entire package the company provides. Research each franchise to assess the services they provide, the value of the brand name, and the quality of the training, business, and operations you'll get for your money.

The franchise fee is only the tip of the cost iceberg. It's what you pay to become a member of the club, but that's about it. Depending on the franchise, the franchise fee may or may not include training and support. Sometimes that's extra. Everything else to start up your franchise is usually at your expense—the lease on the building, any necessary remodeling, equipment and supplies, labor costs, permits, taxes, and other operational costs.

QUICK TIP

When a Bargain Isn't a Good Deal

A low franchise fee is not always a great deal. It may mean many things. It may be that there is little or no demand for the franchise, since it is an unproven concept. It may mean that the franchise has been in trouble and is having difficulties finding new franchisees. It may mean that the franchise provides little or no support, training, or advertising. If a franchise fee is too low for its industry, investigate to discover the cause.

Franchise fees by industry

The chart below shows the minimum, maximum, and average franchise fees for common franchise industries. These numbers come from a 2006 study done by the International Franchise Association and FranData. (Where no minimum is listed, data was not available.)

INDUSTRY	MINIMUM FEE	MAXIMUM FEE	AVERAGE FEE
Automotive		$1,000,000	$25,000
Baked goods	$7,500	$80,000	$30,000
Building/Construction		$200,000	$25,000
Business services	$1,000	$500,000	$25,000
Child-related	$2,000	$270,000	$23,500
Education-related	$500	$190,000	$19,500
Fast food		$75,000	$25,000
Lodging	$5,000	$125,000	$35,000
Maintenance services	$500	$500,000	$26,000
Personnel services	$5,000	$1,000,000	$17,000
Printing	$3,500	$44,500	$25,000
Real estate		$400,000	$16,900
Restaurants	$9,500	$250,000	$35,000
Retail food		$275,000	$26,500
Retail		$135,000	$25,000
Service businesses	$500	$1,000,000	$25,000
Sports & recreation	$3,500	$350,000	$28,500
Travel		$30,000	$20,000

Royalties

The royalty fee is an ongoing expense you have to pay your franchisor every month, based on a percentage of gross sales, for the life of your franchise. It is, in most cases, how franchisors make their money. Royalty fees usually range anywhere from 5% to 12% of gross sales, but the higher fees (above 10%) also usually include advertising and marketing services from the franchisor. If the royalty fees don't include advertising and marketing, expect to pay an additional 2% average on an ongoing basis for advertising and marketing help from the franchisor, if they provide these services. The royalty fees and advertising fees combined should not be above 12% to 14%. If they are, you're paying too much.

With any franchise, the royalty fees are used to pay expenses, help the franchise make a profit, and expand the franchise. But with a worthwhile franchise, the royalty fees are also used to provide effective training, ongoing support for franchisees, research and development of new products, and technology upgrades. In other words, the fees are used to help benefit the entire franchise system, including the training and support of franchisees. In a less desirable franchise, the royalty money is used mostly to help sell more franchises without providing the necessary training and support to existing franchisees. You'll learn more about how to tell a worthwhile franchise from a not-so-worthwhile one in Section 5, The UFOC and Franchise Agreement, and Section 6, Due Diligence.

Established and successful franchises do not negotiate royalty fees. The fees are stated in the UFOC and if a franchisor changed these fees for you, they would have to change them for everyone and restate the amount in an updated UFOC. However, many franchisors offer incentives to their successful franchisees in the form of reduced royalty fees after several years of successful operation. For example, a franchisor may reduce its royalty fees from 7% to 6% after you have operated according to their policies for five years.

Royalty fees are usually paid monthly, and they are based on your previous month's gross sales. If you don't pay on time, most franchisors will charge you a late fee. In addition, your franchisor has the right to audit your books, and if they discover you've underreported your sales, you'll be required to pay for the audit in addition to penalties and the unpaid royalties.

Some franchisors require a minimum royalty regardless of actual sales, and some will require you to continue paying royalties for the life of your agreement, even if you default or go out of business early. This is another reason that it's important to have an experienced attorney carefully review your franchise agreement before you sign it.

Not all franchisors charge royalty fees. But if they don't, they are not necessarily offering a good deal. The franchisor may charge a huge franchise fee up front and then provide no ongoing support or they may require that you buy all supplies from them at a large markup. Other franchisors may charge a flat royalty fee, rather than a percentage of your gross sales. This could be beneficial to you when sales are up, but not so good when sales are poor. Flat-rate royalties also generally mean less ongoing support from the franchisor.

QUICK TIP

Consider the Costs

When you're calculating your startup expenses, be sure to factor in the income you'll be giving up while starting a franchise. If you're leaving a job with health insurance, you'll have to purchase this on your own. If the franchisor requires you to go to a two-week training program at company headquarters, there will be travel and accommodation expenses and no salary during that period. Some established franchises even require you to work as a manager in their system for six months to a year before becoming a franchise owner, possibly reducing your income during this period.

Startup costs

The franchise fee is the first payment you'll make toward starting your franchise. Your *total initial investment* will cover the rest of the costs to get your business going. These costs will include your lease expenses (such as first and last month's rent and security deposits); build-out or remodeling needed for an outlet; equipment, supplies, and inventory to run the business for the first three months; and all necessary insurance and business permits. Other expenses could include signage, advertising, and marketing expenses for the grand opening, as well as working capital for the first three months.

Total initial investments for acquiring a franchise vary widely, depending on the type of franchise you choose, where it's located, and other factors. The cost of leasing a building, for example, is far greater in certain parts of the country than in others. Total startup costs for a franchise can be very expensive. But keep in mind that these costs will be financed. Typically, you will have to come up with at least 20% to 30% of the total, and the rest will be financed by a lender. (See pages 148-160 for more on financing.)

If you're acquiring a franchise that needs a storefront, you'll have to find and pay for a suitable location. Most franchise systems (apart from hotel and motel franchises) do not require you to purchase property or buildings. Whether it's purchased or leased, you're responsible for remodeling your space to the franchisor's specifications.

Major startup costs include:

■ **Training.** Well-run franchisors provide training at their headquarters to teach you their business and operational systems. This training usually lasts one to two weeks. Travel to and from the headquarters, hotel accommodation, and meals are often at your expense (and some franchises also charge for the classes). You will not usually have to pay for ongoing training when new products or services are introduced, but you will usually have to pay for ongoing training (if needed) to help you with the everyday operations of your business.

■ **Leasing store, kiosk, or vehicle.** You rarely have to buy land or buildings to start a franchise. The exception is hotel and motel franchises, which often require land acquisition and development. Sometimes the franchisor owns the building and you lease from them. Otherwise, you'll lease your own space, the location of which is usually subject to the approval of your franchisor. Look for a 5-year lease with multiple options to renew. You should have enough capital set aside to pay at least the first three months' rent.

■ **Build-out costs.** If it doesn't already conform to your franchisor's specifications, you'll be responsible for remodeling or improving the building to fit the franchisor's requirements. Also included here are the costs of the equipment you need to run your business. You must know exactly what these build-out requirements include before you sign up for the franchise, because a big expense could be involved.

■ **Initial inventory.** These are the supplies and products you need for the first three months of business. You may not have a choice about the supplier from whom you'll purchase your supplies. Some franchisors require you to buy directly from them, and if not, most have a list of approved suppliers for you to choose from.

■ **Grand opening marketing.** The marketing of your grand opening is usually done at your expense. It does not come out of the general advertising fund or the monthly advertising fee you pay. The cost will vary, depending on the type of franchise and how big a "splash" you're attempting to make with your opening. Spending $500 on grand opening marketing would be considered a very modest amount. Spending $10,000 would be considered a serious commitment to your opening.

Buying Power

Nationwide franchises give you the advantage of national buying power, and volume purchases mean discounted prices. In many cases, you can acquire the equipment you need to run your business for less than you would if you bought it as an independent business from the same suppliers.

However, national buying power will not necessarily mean the cheapest prices for supplies, because franchisors want you to buy from approved suppliers to maintain consistency and quality. For example, if you have a pizza franchise, you might be able to get mozzarella cheese at a lower price from a local supplier than from the approved supplier. But you're not allowed to do so because the franchisor can't guarantee the consistency of a non-approved supplier's product. Some franchisors also mark up the cost of supplies as a part of their business model.

- **Working capital** is cash available to operate your business until it starts turning a profit. This will take a minimum of three months, but more likely a year and maybe much longer than that.

- **Uniforms, other clothing, and miscellaneous expenses.** These include any signage, landscaping, attorney and accountant fees, licenses, permits, uniforms, other clothing, and other expenses.

Total initial investment by industry

This chart (using data compiled by FranData in 2006 for the International Franchise Association) shows the range of total initial investment for various franchise industries.

INDUSTRY	TYPICAL LOW-END COST	TYPICAL HIGH-END COST
Automotive	$150,000	$285,000
Baked goods	$210,000	$395,000
Building/Construction	$71,000	$148,000
Business services	$51,000	$84,000
Child-related	$78,000	$154,000
Education-related	$36,000	$75,000
Fast food	$178,000	$2,900,000
Lodging	$4,100,000	$6,500,000
Maintenance services	$39,500	$92,500
Personnel services	$74,000	$150,000
Printing	$172,500	$278,000
Real estate	$31,000	$98,300
Restaurants	$423,000	$920,000
Retail food	$152,000	$318,000
Retail	$129,500	$249,000
Service businesses	$65,000	$136,000
Sports & recreation	$4,500	$340,000
Travel	$68,000	$135,000

Think Mobile

The numbers in the chart on page 84 show typical startup costs for franchises that operate in a store or office location. If you run a business out of your home or have a mobile franchise, you'll save a lot. When you acquire a mobile service franchise, such as a carpet-cleaning or mobile oil-change service, you won't have a building to lease or improve. Instead, you'll need to purchase or lease the business vehicle and obtain insurance for it, as well as paying for equipment, supply, and advertising costs.

Imagine you're joining a mobile computer-repair franchise. In this business, you do on-site computer repairs, upgrades, or servicing. A typical total initial investment for this franchise would be about $61,000, and it would include:

- **Franchise fee:** $25,000

- **Advertising fee:** $15,000 for initial cost to cover the first three months of advertising (and $275 per week after that)

- **Initial supplies:** $3,000–$5,000 for supplies, equipment, uniforms, marketing materials, and other printed materials needed to run your business

- **Working capital:** $16,000, including the purchase or lease of a vehicle, licenses and permits, insurance, training expenses, and additional working capital for the startup period

Other mobile franchises have similar costs. If you're starting a mobile pet-grooming service, for example, the typical total initial investment, including franchise fee, advertising, initial supplies, and working capital, would be $45,000 to $65,000.

QUICK TIP

Buy Used and Save

Depending on the type of franchise you're acquiring, you may not need brand-new equipment to run a successful business. You can save substantially by buying used equipment. If you have a restaurant franchise, you can buy pre-owned commercial ovens and sinks for a fraction of the cost of new ones. But check with your franchisor to make certain you are allowed to purchase used equipment.

Ongoing costs

Along with franchise fees and royalty payments, you'll be responsible for a number of other startup and ongoing costs, large and small. These will range from the expense of equipment and utilities to such things as business licenses, insurance costs, and ongoing fees such as advertising fees. You may also be responsible for the costs of audits, employee healthcare, and improvements.

The following chart outlines some of the fees you are likely to encounter.

COST	WHAT IT IS	WILL I HAVE TO PAY IT?	WATCH OUT FOR
Franchise fee	The amount you pay to acquire the rights to the franchise	Yes	Most franchise fees include some training and support. If the fee includes no services, a low franchise fee is not a bargain.
Royalty payments	An ongoing fee to the franchisor, paid as either a flat amount or as a percentage of income	Yes, and it's usually 4% to 12% of gross, not net, income.	You may have to pay royalties even if you're not turning a profit. Read the fine print.
Training and support	The initial training to get you up to speed on how to operate the franchise. Support comes in the form of ongoing help and troubleshooting.	Maybe. Training and/or support could be included in the franchise fee.	Some franchisors charge extra for ongoing training and support after the initial training.
Utilities, phone, security	Gas, electric, phone, water, surveillance systems or security guards.	Yes	Depending on your franchise and location, utilities can be a large expense.
Improvements	Work done to your place of business to make it conform to the look and quality standards of the franchise.	Yes	Find out before you sign the agreement exactly what these improvements are. This could be a big expense.
Equipment	The equipment and hardware you need to run your franchise.	Yes	You may be obligated to purchase equipment from the franchisor.

COST	WHAT IT IS	WILL I HAVE TO PAY IT?	WATCH OUT FOR
Supplies/Inventory	The materials you need to operate your business.	Yes	You may be required to purchase supplies only from the franchisor—and at a higher price than you could get from other vendors.
Taxes	Local, state, and federal taxes, as required by law.	Yes	You know what they say about death and taxes.
Land purchase/ Building construction	Land purchase and construction from scratch. (Required for hotel/ motel franchises.)	Rarely	Property prices vary widely across the country and may be prohibitively expensive.
Rent or lease	Lease on a building used for business.	Yes	You may be required to rent or lease your business from the franchisor.
Licenses/Permits	Various business licenses and permits required.	Yes	Vary from state to state and city to city.
Insurance	General liability insurance, including product liability, as well as property insurance or auto insurance, if there's a company car or mobile unit.	Yes	The franchisor usually requires a minimum stated amount (for example, $1 million) of liability insurance.
Accountant	Accountants determine the franchise's earnings potential and what you can afford—and advise you on your business plan.	Yes	Hire an accountant who has worked on franchises before.
Attorney	Franchise attorney reviews UFOC and franchise agreement and a real estate attorney reviews lease.	Yes	Hire attorneys who have experience in these fields.
Grand opening or promotion fees	Includes all the advertising and marketing to announce your outlet's opening.	Yes	Can be a large one-time expense.

Continued

COST	WHAT IT IS	WILL I HAVE TO PAY IT?	WATCH OUT FOR
Renewal fees	Fee paid to franchisor when term of first agreement ends (typically 10 years) and you want to sign a new franchise agreement.	Yes	Negotiate the fee amount when you sign the first agreement. There's no guarantee that the franchisor will renew your contract at the same fee as the initial agreement.
Bookkeeping, payroll, bill paying	These are essential ongoing business activities.	You do them or pay someone else to do them.	
Audits	Franchisor has the right to check your books, accounting, and tax returns as spelled out in the franchise agreement.	Sometimes	You pay audit fees if you do not send your franchisor required information or reports or if they find you have understated your gross sales. There may be other penalties for non-compliance.
Advertising	National, regional, and local advertising.	Yes (% fee to franchisor)	Required to pay into a general advertising fund, even if your particular franchise isn't promoted.
Transfer fee	A fee paid to the franchisor when you want to sell your franchise to a new owner.	Yes	This should not be too expensive ($3,000 is average) and even less if you want to transfer ownership to a spouse or child.
Workers' compensation/ Health insurance	Depending on franchise, ongoing expense for employees.	Yes	You may need to offer health coverage to attract and keep good employees.
Working capital	Money set aside to run company during the first year of operation or until it becomes profitable.	Yes	Set aside enough to pay bills for at least 6 months and preferably one year.
Other professional fees	If modifying a building to fit your franchisor's standard, you'll need an architect or civil engineer.	Yes	The franchisor sometimes provides a set of standard architectural plans.

The Lease You Should Know

A favorable, long-term lease is essential to the success of a franchise. After all, having to move to a new location after a year or two could be devastating to your franchise. Or if your rent suddenly doubles or triples, your franchise could go from profitable to unprofitable. To make sure you are protected:

- Enlist the services of a commercial real estate agent to help find the location and negotiate the lease.

- Have an experienced *real estate* attorney review the lease before you sign it. Franchise attorneys don't always have expertise in property or real estate law.

- Avoid a 10-year lease to start out. If your business fails or you decide to move, you'll be liable for the remainder of the lease if another suitable tenant isn't found. Look for a 5-year lease, with multiple options to renew (every 5 years, up to a total of 20 years). If you decide to vacate the premises at one of the 5-year intervals, you will be able to do so without penalty.

- Know your window of opportunity to renew. Typically, leases have provisions that require you to notify the landlord 6 months before the lease expires if you want to exercise your option to renew.

- Negotiate the terms of renewal at the beginning of your first lease. Typically, you'll get one of two types of renewals. One is a flat rate. If you have a 5-year flat rate lease, at the beginning of the 61st month, you'll start paying the new rate. You know what your rent will be, and you can plan for it.

With the second type of renewal, the rent goes to whatever the market rate is at the time of renewal. This can be beneficial to you if rental rates in your area are stable or rise slowly, but it can work against you if you live in an area of rapidly escalating rents.

- Your franchisor may require certain provisions in your lease. For example, they may insist that they be able to take over your lease if you default so they can keep the franchise going. They may also want to make sure your lease gives you the option of keeping the property for at least the length of your franchise agreement.

- You may be required to lease from your franchisor because they own the property. If that is the case, check to see that you're paying market rate and getting the same protections that you'd get from any other landlord.

How Much Will You Make?

Earnings Claims or Empty Claims?

Earnings claims are often not enlightening. There are so many disclaimers and they're usually broad enough and vague enough to not be very helpful. That's why you're better off calling other franchisees.

Peter Chase,
Franchise and Business Attorney,
Boston, Massachusetts

Where's the Beef?

Net profit statements on company-owned outlets are misleading because these outlets have lower costs than franchisees. They can buy equipment and supplies more cheaply because of economies of scale, and they may own the property, so they won't have rent and leasing expenses.

The first question most potential franchisees ask is: How much money will I make? But this is rarely the first question franchisors answer. The amount of money you can expect to make is called an "earnings claim" on the UFOC. While this item appears on every UFOC, franchisors are not required to fill it in—and only 14% do. So it's unlikely the franchise you're interested in will offer an exact statement—*in writing*—of what you can expect to earn.

There are a number of reasons why franchisors are reluctant to make claims about the net sales and profits of their franchises. They don't want to be sued by franchisees who follow the system but don't make as much money as the earnings claims state they will. They recognize that some markets are likely to be more successful than others. And some franchisees turn out to be better businesspeople than others.

All the same, franchisors may make some earnings claims. Overeager franchise salespeople may give you optimistic projections verbally. Franchisors may also provide a list of franchise gross sales without indicating which franchisees have earned that amount. These figures are usually based on a group of franchises bunched together, and many may have been open for a long period of time or they may be in particularly advantageous locations.

Even if the franchise you're considering is one of the few that makes an earnings claim, don't assume your outlet will achieve the same success. Do additional research, including market research in your region, analyze industry statistics, and talk to existing and former franchisees to find out how much you can expect to make.

When a franchisor makes an earnings claim:

- If the claim is made orally only (meaning it's not in the UFOC), get it in writing.

- Find out what the earnings claim is based on. Is it based on the average earnings of all its franchises? Or is it just a projection with no real franchisee numbers to back it up? If it's based on the average of all franchises in the system, make sure the numbers are from franchised outlets and not from company-owned stores.

- Find out whether the earnings claim was prepared by an independent certified public accountant. If so, verify that the CPA did the earnings claim according to the American Institute of Certified Public Accountants Standards for Financial Forecasts or Projections.

- Read the disclaimers relating to the earnings claim. These disclaimers may make the claims virtually useless. For example, the earnings claims could be based on the financial performances of a few well-performing franchises in hot markets, not a typical franchise in the system.

- Get information about both *net* profits and *gross* income. Gross sales may look great, but these figures won't tell you whether franchisees are actually making any profits. Huge costs and franchisee royalties and fees could mean that a franchise is in the red even when it has impressive gross sales.

- Ask the franchisor to provide net profit information on its franchisees, not on its company-owned outlets.

- Talk to other franchisees in your region or in comparable markets to find out their net income and how long it took them to turn a profit.

Do the Math

If you can't get gross sales numbers from the franchisor or from franchisees you talk to, you can still figure out the average sales per outlet by using the following formula. Remember that the results will just be *average* numbers and that they may be made a lot higher by the great performance of a few stores.

1. Franchisors are required to include in the UFOC an audited financial statement covering the previous three years of their business. Under "Revenues," look for "Franchise Royalties." This number represents the total royalties received in the years covered.

2. Subtract the number of company-owned outlets from the total number of outlets. Corporate-owned outlets don't pay royalties.

3. Divide the total royalty payment by the number of franchised outlets. This will give you the average royalty payment per outlet.

4. Divide the average royalty payment per outlet by the royalty rate the franchise requires (for example, if it's 7%, divide by .07.) This will give you the average gross sales per outlet, since royalty payments are based on gross sales.

Full Disclosure

"The UFOC is one of the most detailed disclosure documents in any area of the law. It's designed to help the little guy. And that's good. But the point is, the little guy's got to read it."

Peter Chase,
Franchise and Business Attorney,
Boston, Massachusetts

The UFOC *and* Franchise Agreement

The Uniform Franchise Offering Circular (UFOC)

The four most important letters in any franchisee's alphabet are UFOC (Uniform Franchise Offering Circular). Also known as the "offering circular," the UFOC is a *disclosure document* that the U.S. Federal Trade Commission (FTC) requires all franchisors to give to potential franchisees. It is not the franchise agreement, which is the contract the franchisee negotiates and signs with the franchisor. The UFOC discloses initial franchise fees, franchisee and franchisor obligations to each other, limits on products and services, financing, financial statements, dispute resolution, litigation or bankruptcy proceedings against the franchise, and much more.

It's important to understand what the UFOC does — and what it does not do. The UFOC requires certain disclosures on the part of the franchisor. This means the franchisor must give prospective franchisees certain

QUICK TIP

Hire a Franchise Attorney

The *type* of information you'll find on a UFOC is standardized. The *actual* information provided, however, is far from uniform. Obligations and costs vary widely from franchise to franchise. Take the time to read any UFOC thoroughly and, most importantly, hire an experienced franchise attorney to review its provisions so you'll avoid unpleasant surprises down the road.

information. However, the government does not review this information and/or certify that the information on the UFOC is true. If you later discover that some of the disclosures on the UFOC are false, your only option is to sue the franchisor. The government will not take action on your behalf. The Federal Trade Commission (FTC) doesn't check any of the information on a UFOC, and it doesn't recommend any particular franchises.

There's a very good reason behind the creation of the UFOC. While many excellent franchises have always been available, numerous scam artists and unethical operators have also been at work. In 1978, the FTC stepped in and required franchisors to provide details about their business opportunities in a document called the UFOC. In 1995, this requirement was strengthened with a demand for more stringent disclosures. The UFOC is now a federal requirement, used in every state in the U.S. Some states require additional disclosures, as well.

The FTC mandates the franchisor to give the franchisee the UFOC at the first face-to-face meeting with the franchisor. It also requires that the franchisee will receive this document at least 10 business days before making any payment or signing a contract to acquire a franchise. This is to protect the franchisee from making a rash buying decision by requiring a cooling-off period, during which the franchisee can look at the numbers, absorb the information, and do additional research.

The UFOC clearly lists all your costs as franchisee and all your responsibilities, as well as all the franchisor's responsibilities. It gives you the background of the executives at the franchise you're considering and it lists all the other franchisees and how to contact them. After examining the UFOC, you'll have a much better idea about whether you want to proceed or not.

The UFOC is not the contract you sign when you buy a franchise. That is called the franchise agreement, and it

Put $$ in the Margins

I suggest that when you're going through the UFOC, you put $$ signs in the margins whenever you see a place they'll charge you. It can start to add up. Besides the royalty and advertising fees, there are a number of places they can nickel and dime you. Sometimes they make you sublease or charge you extra setup fees. Sometimes you have to buy a certain amount of product, or all your supplies, from the franchisor. That can be an extra income stream for them.

Peter Chase,
Franchise and Business Attorney,
Boston, Massachusetts

is usually attached to the back of the UFOC as part of Item 22 (see page 101). The franchise agreement is a much shorter document than the UFOC, but the terms listed in the franchise agreement with regard to costs and responsibilities should be the same as those in the UFOC.

It cannot be stated often enough: Have an experienced franchise attorney review both the UFOC and the franchise agreement and give you advice before you proceed. You don't negotiate the UFOC; it is just an information document. If there are changes you want to negotiate to your terms, you do that with the franchise agreement.

The UFOC: Item by item

The UFOC consists of 23 separate numbered sections called "Items." All franchisors must follow this format, so Item 5, for instance, is always the "Initial franchise fee." The following chart lists all 23 items in the UFOC, shows what is contained in each item, and reveals some of the critical things to look for when reviewing the document.

Quick Tip

Straight to the Numbers

To go straight to the places that tell you how much it will cost you to become a franchisee, look at Items 5, 6, and 7. After learning the "Initial franchise fee" in Item 5, you'll find "Other fees" in Item 6 and "Initial investment" in Item 7. Remember: Costs will be given as a range of figures, rather than a definitive number. And the cost of building and improvements will depend on where your franchise is located.

UFOC ITEM NO.	WHAT'S IN THIS ITEM	LOOK FOR
FTC cover page	A letter from the FTC disclosing that they have not verified the information in the UFOC and do not know whether it is correct or not. The FTC neither approves nor recommends any franchise. The FTC strongly recommends that you have an attorney or an accountant review the UFOC for you. Follow this advice.	Because the UFOC is an official-looking document, people sometimes assume the FTC has verified the information in it. Don't make this mistake. This page lists the date the disclosure document was issued or last updated. If it's even just a few months old, ask for updated information, such as a list of new litigation, new financial statements, or any names of franchisees that have recently left the system.
State registration page	Lists requirements for franchise registration states. (See list of registration states on page 101.)	Some states provide extra protection for franchisees, such as requiring franchisors to show good cause before terminating a franchisee. Contact the state agency to see if any complaints have been filed against the franchise.
Item 1: The franchisor, its predecessors, and affiliates	The company's name, address, and state of incorporation—and the type of product or service it offers. Names of predecessors and affiliates are also included. Reveals whether company has offered franchises under a different name.	If the company has changed its name several times, find out why. It could be because of bankruptcies or legal problems.
Item 2: Business experience	Information about directors, officers, board members, and executives for the past 5 years.	Look for a company whose owners and managers have franchise operational experience.
Item 3: Litigation history	Pending or past legal proceedings, investigations, or convictions, including criminal and civil litigation.	Check to see whether key executives have been convicted of crimes or whether there are rulings against the franchise by courts or arbiters. Some litigation in medium or large franchises isn't unusual. But if there is a total of 20 franchisees and 10 have sued, that's cause for concern.
Item 4: Bankruptcy	Bankruptcies of the franchise or its officers, predecessors, and affiliates in the past 10 years.	A bankruptcy can hurt a franchisor's ability to borrow money, which impacts the company's future growth.
Item 5: Initial franchise fee	Franchise fee amount and whether it's due in one lump sum or installments. If the franchise fee is not standardized, the range of franchise fees and the formula for determining the fee are provided.	Franchise fees are usually non-refundable, but there are conditions under which some franchisors will refund the fee. For example, some franchises will refund the franchise fee within 30 days of signing the agreement if you decide to back out or within 30 days of completion of training.

Continued

UFOC ITEM NO.	WHAT'S IN THIS ITEM	LOOK FOR
Item 6: Other fees	Lists royalty fees, fees for advertising, additional training, audits, accounting, inventory, transfers, renewals, tax mediation and attorney fees, and any other services for which the franchisor charges.	Many franchisors require a minimum royalty, regardless of actual sales. If the franchise has no royalty fee, check for a large markup on supplies. Flat-rate royalties usually mean less ongoing support.
Item 7: Initial investment	Startup costs, including franchise fee, training costs, lease, real estate improvements, equipment and fixtures, signs, decorating, opening inventory, initial advertising, security deposits, utility deposits, business licenses and permits, and additional working capital for the first 3 months of operation.	In addition to the approximate cost of each item, the chart tells you the method of payment (one lump sum or installments), when the initial investment is due, whether it's refundable, and to whom the payment is made.
Item 8: Restrictions on sources of products and services	Products and services you have to buy and sources from which you must buy them. Specifications for products and services are included, as well as any volume discount programs.	If the franchisor is the sole supplier of goods and services, make sure the prices are in line with what a competitor would charge. If the franchisor makes money on product sales to you, a good franchisor will tell you how much in this item, though there is no requirement for the franchisor to do so. Look at the franchisor's new vendor policy to see how difficult it is to get new vendors approved. Also, where are the required vendors located? Transportation and shipping costs can be very expensive if the vendors are on the other side of the country.
Item 9: Franchisee's obligations	List of franchisee's obligations: site selection, lease or acquisition, initial and ongoing training, opening requirements and dates, fees, compliance with standards and policies, restrictions on products and services, customer service requirements, territorial development, sales quotas, ongoing product/services purchases, maintenance, insurance, advertising, owner's participation in management, records and reports, inspections and audits, transfers, renewals, post-termination obligations, non-competition covenants, and dispute resolution.	Review each obligation thoroughly with a franchise attorney. These are important obligations. You will have to understand the costs involved and the limits they place on your operating flexibility. Although the UFOC is for information only, the information about the franchisor's policies in the UFOC should be the same as the information in the franchise agreement. Negotiate, when possible, for more favorable terms. (See pages 107-108 for what can be negotiated.) (The franchise agreement should be included at the back of the UFOC as part of Item 22. If it's not, the franchisor will send it to you separately.)

UFOC ITEM NO.	WHAT'S IN THIS ITEM	LOOK FOR
Item 10: Financing	Financing terms (interest, repayment periods, personal guarantees) are spelled out in this item.	If the franchisor offers financing, compare your loan with the financing offered to other franchisees and available from other sources. The lender, whether it's the franchisor or other sources, will almost certainly ask you to sign a personal guarantee on the loan. Even if you have formed a corporation to protect your assets, check to see whether you're personally liable for repaying the loan.
Item 11: Franchisor's obligations	List of franchisor's obligations: site selection and development, leasing, advertising, training programs, register and computer systems. Marketing and advertising are included in Item 11 if the franchisor provides these services (and you'll usually be paying a percentage of your gross sales for these services).	Pay attention to the training and advertising programs. Training programs should be comprehensive and include follow-up visits to your franchise by trainers. If you need help finding a good location and negotiating a lease, get it in writing here. This item also includes information about the franchisor's advertising and marketing plans (if they have such plans), including the minimum amounts they will spend on them.
Item 12: Territory	Indicates whether there is an exclusive territory and how large it is. The method for conflict resolution regarding territorial rights is included here, as well as the right to modify the territory in the future.	If you don't meet certain revenue minimums or other performance standards, some franchisors can force you to share your territory with another franchisee or can even terminate your franchise. If there's no guarantee of exclusive or protected territory, the franchisor could put another franchisee next door.
Item 13: Trademarks	Discloses whether franchisor owns its trademark and which trademarks are licensed to the franchisee. The item also describes any limits on use of trademarks.	The franchisor's trademark must be federally registered and used continuously for at least five years to be incontestable. If your franchise doesn't have that, it's not as valuable as a franchise that does.
Item 14: Patents, copyrights, and proprietary information	Reveals whether franchisor has a patented system that makes it unique and terms and conditions for use of trade secrets (such as their "secret sauce").	Look for franchises that have a patented product or service that is truly unique and in demand.
Item 15: Participation in the actual operation of the franchise	Item 15 specifies whether you have to be an active, hands-on owner or whether you can be an absentee owner and hire a manager to run the store.	Most franchisors require absentee owners to send managers to training (paid for by the franchisee) and some require that the managers maintain a part-ownership in the franchise.

Continued

UFOC ITEM NO.	WHAT'S IN THIS ITEM	LOOK FOR
Item 16: Restrictions on what the franchisee may sell	Details products and services to offer to customers and any limits to, or conditions on, those sales.	Recognize the limits on your ability to change or modify what you sell, even if there is demand for different products or services in your local market.
Item 17: Renewal, termination, transfers, and dispute resolution	Details terms of renewals, terminations, transfers, and dispute resolution. Item 17 includes when renewals may be made and how many may be made, reasons franchisor may terminate agreement, and how long franchisee has to fix ("cure") problems before franchisor can terminate agreement.	Make sure you have at least a 30-day "right to cure" any violations of the franchise agreement before the franchisor can terminate the agreement. Build in automatic renewal provisions. Otherwise, if you aren't guaranteed the right to renew your contract, you can build a franchise location only to have the company refuse to renew your agreement. Dispute resolution takes place in the franchisor's headquarters state, which can become costly. Disputes settled by arbitration favor franchisors, making an arbitration clause attractive.
Item 18: Public figures	If a celebrity or public figure is used to promote a franchise, the extent of the celebrity's involvement and the amount they're paid is listed here.	A celebrity's involvement doesn't guarantee success. Check to see whether the celebrity is paid an endorsement or has actually invested in the franchise.
Item 19: Earnings claims	How much you'll make based on what other franchisees have made. The FTC doesn't require franchisors to provide this estimate, and the majority of them don't.	Even if the franchisor makes an earnings claim, the numbers may be so broad that they're not helpful. A few franchises that perform very well can skew the numbers. Find out whether an independent certified public accountant prepared the claims and whether they were prepared in accordance with the American Institute of CPAs' standards.
Item 20: Other franchisees or company-owned outlets	Total number of franchised outlets, with their names, addresses, and phone numbers. Discloses how many units have been transferred or terminated in the past 3 years. Also included are company-owned outlets, the number of franchises the franchisor plans to sell the following year, and franchise outlets that were not renewed or were reacquired by the franchisor.	You get the best and most realistic information about your future franchise from other franchisees. If there has been a significant percentage of franchise terminations, cancellations, or non-renewals, proceed with caution. Be sure to call as many current and former franchisees as you can and ask the questions starting on page 128.

UFOC ITEM NO.	WHAT'S IN THIS ITEM	LOOK FOR
Item 21: Financial statements	Audited financial statements for the past 3 years (or for as long as the franchise has been in business if less than 3 years).	Use an experienced franchise CPA to review figures provided and evaluate the financial health of the franchise. Be extremely cautious about franchises that are not in good financial health or have failed to file audited financial statements.
Item 22: Contracts	The franchise agreement and any other related agreements, contracts, or licenses are attached as exhibits to the UFOC. These include leases, options, purchase agreements, and financing documents.	The terms of the franchise agreement should not conflict with the terms described in the UFOC. As with the UFOC, have a good franchise attorney carefully review the franchise agreement and all other contracts and agreements.
Item 23: Receipt	You'll sign this page to acknowledge that you've received the UFOC. There are two copies: one for you and one for the franchisor.	Signing this receipt doesn't obligate you to do anything. It's to satisfy the FTC requirement that you've received the UFOC in a timely manner.

Registration States

In addition to the FTC requirements for the UFOC, 15 states call for franchises to separately register and file with them. Some of these states have disclosure requirements or other rules beyond what is required by the FTC. The states in question are: California, Hawaii, Illinois, Indiana, Maryland, Michigan, Minnesota, New York, North Dakota, Oregon, Rhode Island, South Dakota, Virginia, Washington, and Wisconsin.

Several U.S. states have laws that offer additional protection to franchisees, whether or not they are in a registration state. In Delaware, for example, there is a Franchise Security Law that compels franchisors to have good cause for termination and non-renewal of franchisees.

The fact that a franchisor is able to offer a franchise in a registration state does not mean the franchise is better than any other franchise. The states don't recommend particular franchises any more than the FTC does.

The Franchise Agreement

Negotiation

Most terms are not negotiable, but franchisors may change the terms of the agreement if they're young and hungry. It's supply and demand.

Mario Herman, Franchise Attorney, Adamstown, Maryland

The franchise agreement and the Uniform Franchise Offering Circular (UFOC) are not the same. The franchise agreement is the legally binding agreement you'll make with the franchisor. You'll live by this agreement, no matter what it says in the UFOC. The franchise agreement is where the rubber meets the road.

The franchise agreement contains all the information in the UFOC that pertains to your rights and responsibilities and the rights and responsibilities of the franchisor. It differs from the UFOC in that it's a contract, whereas the UFOC is an information document. The franchise agreement also differs from the UFOC in that it does not contain the background information found in the UFOC—things like the company's history, history of company bankruptcy and litigation, earnings claims, and list of outlets and other franchisees.

The franchise agreement normally comes attached to the back of the UFOC as a separate document. It covers all of your initial fees, the terms of your initial and ongoing training, continuing fees such as royalties, restrictions and guidelines on purchasing products and supplies, territorial rights, marketing, advertising and signage agreements, financial reporting and audits, insurance requirements, terms of renewal, termination and transfer, rules of dispute resolution, and much more.

The franchise agreement is often written in "legal-ese." So don't attempt to read and understand a franchise contract by yourself. Have an experienced franchise attorney review both the UFOC and your franchise agreement before you sign anything. Your attorney will review both documents and look for any discrepancies between them. If you don't already have an experienced attorney, the International Franchise Association (IFA) and the American Association of Franchisees and Dealers (AAFD) have resources to help you locate one.

By law, you must have the franchise agreement for at least 5 days before you sign it. This time can run concurrently with the 10 days you have the UFOC before you sign up, but your franchise selection and due diligence are more likely to take months than days. In all cases, take plenty of time to review every written document with your franchise attorney.

Before you sign, make sure:

■ All the terms you've discussed with the franchisor or their representative should now be in writing in the franchise agreement. Remember: If verbal promises are not in the written agreement, the franchisor has no legal obligation to honor them.

■ If anything in the franchise agreement conflicts with the UFOC, find out why and make sure you understand and approve any differences. The terms of the agreement must reflect what you have agreed to and expect to abide by.

Negotiating

Many franchisors are reluctant to make major changes to a standard agreement. Significant changes require them to re-file their UFOC with the Federal Trade Commission (FTC), which takes time and can slow down business. Also, if they make major changes for you, they'd have to make them for other franchisees. Moreover, a good franchise will already have a successful model in place for their operation. And they'll want you to follow it.

There's another, simple reason why successful, mature franchisors don't negotiate much: They don't have to. Franchising is very popular, and successful franchises often have people lining up to join. They can be choosy about whom they accept and can dictate the terms they want. Younger, hungrier franchisors are more eager to sign up new franchisees, so they are usually more willing to negotiate on terms than older ones.

Most items in a successful franchisor's agreement are not negotiable. But agreements are not a completely take-it-or-leave-it proposition either. Some things *are* negotiable, and you'll never know which ones until you try. It never hurts to ask for changes in your favor. The worst the franchisor will do is say no.

Do not try to negotiate the franchise agreement on your own. An experienced franchise attorney is your best ally during these negotiations. Not only does an attorney like this bring experience in franchising; they understand the terminology and industry standards and the subtleties of franchise agreements. Moreover, when you want to negotiate tough points, the attorney can be the "bad guy" with the franchisor, preserving your excellent relationship with them.

But keep in mind that while it's a good idea to push for changes, negotiating can backfire if you push too hard. If your attorney plays hardball and your franchisor has a lot of

Quick Tip

Home State Advantage

One area that is *not* negotiable is where you'll litigate serious disagreements with your franchisor. If you have a dispute with your franchisor and end up in court over it, you'll litigate in the franchisor's home state. The laws of their state, not yours, guide the litigation. And you'll have to find a local lawyer and travel to that state.

franchisee applicants to choose from, your franchisor may lose interest if they think you've become too demanding. Some mature franchises are so popular and have so many willing applicants that they don't need to make any changes to their agreement in order to sell franchises.

The negotiation process is a great way to see how the franchisor deals with issues. During the life of your franchise, you'll no doubt need to negotiate or work out further differences with your franchisor. The discussions concerning the franchise agreement will be a good indicator of how the franchisor will deal with situations requiring give and take.

When should you start to negotiate? That depends on the franchise. If it's a well-established franchise brand, you probably won't be negotiating much, if any, of the terms. If it's a young franchise, however, you'll have more leeway, and negotiations can commence when you first receive the UFOC and franchise agreement. (Remember: You negotiate the agreement, not the UFOC.) However, even with a young franchise, you can negotiate only so hard before alienating them. You'll have to use your best judgment to figure how much negotiation is too much.

Don't expect any leeway on the royalty rate in a mature and successful franchise. This is most franchisors' major income stream and if they changed it for you, by law they'd have to change it for all their franchisees. The only exception to this would occur if you happened to be the first or one of the first handful of franchisees. In that case, many aspects of the agreement, including royalty rates, will not have been set in stone yet, and you may have some bargaining power. But in negotiating with an established company with many franchisees, there will be no way to alter the royalty rate.

It may seem at first that it's a good thing for a franchisor to be willing to negotiate on many terms of the agreement. But actually, it's not. Great flexibility on terms usually means one of two things. First, it may mean that the franchise is very young and unproven. This, in turn, means that while you may be getting better terms in your agreement, you will be taking a bigger risk. You'll be getting less in terms of a successful operating system and a proven business model and brand name. A high degree of flexibility could also mean that the franchise is trying to get most of its money from the franchise fee and doesn't really care about your long-term success. These types of franchises offer poor training and support and focus almost entirely on selling new franchises. If you're not getting the operating system and support you need from your franchisor, what is the real value of the arrangement? Reputable franchises maintain consistency throughout their system and therefore are not likely to be flexible in negotiations. That has been a key to their success.

But many parts of the agreement can be changed in your favor without negatively impacting the consistency of the franchise as a whole. For instance, you *can* often negotiate successfully in the so-called "right to cure" your own breaches. This means that if your franchisor finds that you're not in compliance with its standards, you will have a specified amount of time to correct the problem. Without this provision, you could technically be terminated for violating the terms of your agreement, even for minor infractions. With this "right to cure" provision, you will have a specified amount of time, typically 30 days, to fix the problem. Most good franchisors have a provision that enables you to correct violations, but they are not required by law to do this. So if they don't, you should negotiate for it to be included. Practically speaking, most franchisors won't terminate you for a minor breach of their system. They don't want a revolving door of franchisees. More likely, they'll use this provision to make sure you conform more closely to their system.

What to negotiate

Here are some areas where you should be able to negotiate terms in your favor. Nevertheless, individual franchises vary on the degree to which they will negotiate. So use a good franchise attorney to help you negotiate these items:

- **Protected territory.** Negotiate a protected or exclusive territory if one is not automatically provided in the franchise agreement. Or if the protected territory is quite small according to the standard franchise agreement, try to negotiate a larger one. Make sure you are protected not only against other franchisees, but also against company-owned outlets in your territory. Find out what a competitor's franchisor offers. If a competitor's franchisor offers a larger protected territory than your franchisor, use that as a negotiating tool.

- **"Right to cure" your breaches.** If the franchisor finds that you're in violation of any part of their system, this provision will give you a certain amount of time to fix the problem. Try to get at least a 30-day period to correct problems. Without this, the franchisor can technically terminate your contract for any violation.

- **Extra training and support.** Negotiate for training and support in addition to what is provided in the standard franchise agreement. Along with the standard one- or two-week training, for example, negotiate for extra support and training for the grand opening and a follow-up support visit once a month for the first six months.

- **Franchise fee payment schedule.** Instead of paying the entire franchise fee at once, negotiate a down payment and then a payment schedule. If, for example, the franchise fee is $25,000, negotiate to pay half down upon signing the franchise agreement and the rest in installments over a negotiated period of time.

Front-Loaded

The good franchises make their money on the royalties. If you see a franchise agreement that looks front-loaded, if they are making their money on the sale of the franchise and not the royalty, that is cause for concern. By front-loaded I mean a high franchise fee compared to what you have to pay later in royalties. That could be a fly-by-night company trying to take the money and run. You want them to have an investment in your success.

Peter Chase,
Franchise and Business Attorney,
Boston, Massachusetts

- **Opening date for your store.** Your franchisor wants you to open as soon as possible. If you think you need more time to get everything ready for your grand opening, negotiate for more time.

- **Transfer fees and terms.** Negotiate for the ability to transfer your franchise to a new owner for no fee or a nominal fee. Also negotiate that the terms for the new owner will be the same as for you. Otherwise, the franchisor will be able to impose new terms on the new owner, potentially making it more difficult for you to sell.

- **Price for your franchise if you sell.** Franchisors often want the first right to buy back your franchise upon termination or if you want to sell. They have a formula for determining the purchase price that often makes the price significantly lower than what you could get on the open market. To prevent this lowball price from coming into play, negotiate a better formula for determining the price. Sometimes a franchisor will settle for a simple right of first refusal. (A right of first refusal means that they have the right to match any legitimate offer you get from another buyer.)

- **Automatic renewals.** An automatic renewal means that you can automatically renew your franchise agreement at the end of your current term, so long as you have performed your responsibilities adequately. Terms of the renewal are almost always the same as those offered at the time of the first agreement. However, some franchisors offer incentives to their long-term franchisees. For example, your royalty rates may go down from 6% to 5% when you renew after a 10-year term.

- **Your personal guarantee.** Even if you form a corporation to help protect your personal assets from business debts, most franchisors will ask you to sign a "personal guarantee" to meet all your obligations under the franchise agreement. In effect, they'll ask you to "pierce your own corporate veil" and assume personal liability for debts anyway. But a few franchisors are willing to either waive this signing of a personal guarantee or limit your personal liability under the guarantee. Remember: There may still be tax benefits to forming a corporation even if you have to sign the personal guarantee.

Analyze your franchise agreement

The following worksheets will help you analyze the terms of your franchise agreement and determine whether they will be acceptable to you—or which changes you might try to negotiate. If you are satisfied with the way your agreement answers a question, check the first column. Use the second to list any changes you'd like to see in the agreement. Then take your notes to your lawyer when you begin to discuss your negotiation strategy.

Remember: Many franchises are reluctant to make major changes to their standard agreements, so if you find that many of the terms are not acceptable, this may not be the right franchise for you.

Because of franchising's popularity, having too many franchises in a specific area can be a problem. If you don't have an exclusive territory, franchisors can put another franchisee wherever they want, and this could hurt your outlet's sales. That's why it's important to get an exclusive territory, where no other franchisees from your company or company-owned outlets operate.

Some franchisors put provisions into the agreement that change or eliminate exclusivity. For example, franchisors could make your exclusive territory contingent upon reaching certain sales levels. If you fail to arrive at those sales levels, they have the right to take away the exclusive territory and put in an additional franchise. If this provision is included, make sure the sales levels you're being asked to reach are realistic.

Territory and Site Location

LOCATION QUESTIONS	SATISFIED	PROPOSED CHANGES
How close are the nearest competitors?		
How close to my site is the nearest franchisee from the same company?		
Do I have exclusive rights to operate my franchise within a described territory?		
Do I have the right of first refusal to open other company franchises within my area?		
Is the franchisor required to provide help and advice in finding the best location?		
If the lease can't be renewed when it expires, will the franchisor help find another suitable building in the same territory?		
If this is a mobile franchise or a cart, can I go anywhere or are there restrictions on my area of operation?		
If I lose my lease or location through an act of God, may I relocate without penalty?		
Will I have enough time to move?		
Will I be able to stop paying minimum royalties during this period?		

The Lease

LEASE QUESTIONS	SATISFIED	PROPOSED CHANGES
Do I have to lease from the franchisor?		
Are the rent and terms of the lease comparable to other landlords' terms in the area?		
Do I have to pay for utilities, improvements, and property tax increases? If yes, do I know how much this is projected to be?		
Do I have to lease equipment, signs, furniture, or fixtures from the franchisor? If so, are the prices comparable with what another supplier would charge?		

Franchisors sometimes require further improvements or renovations in the future beyond the initial build-out. Suppose your franchisor changes its logo and color scheme one year after you open your store. How much will you have to pay to update your company's identity? Try to negotiate a cap on the amount you'll have to spend for future improvements.

Fees and Royalties

FEES AND ROYALTY QUESTIONS	SATISFIED	PROPOSED CHANGES
What training, services, and support will I get for the initial franchise fee?		
How many hours of training?		
How many hours in the classroom?		
How many visits to my site will a trainer make?		
Will the franchisor finance some or all of the startup costs (inventory, equipment, and property improvements)?		
Can I afford the monthly payments?		
When are the franchise fee and other startup costs due?		
Do I have to pay royalties?		
Are the royalties based on gross sales or net income? Does the franchisor offer a flat-fee royalty instead of a percentage of gross sales?		
How often do I have to pay royalties?		
What do I receive for my royalties?		
Training? Support? Advertising?		
What earnings statements do I have to give to the franchisor and how often?		
Will my advertising fee cover only national advertising or will it also support regional and local advertising?		
Can a marketing or advertising board from the company increase my fee at a later date?		
What do I pay if I default or terminate my contract?		

The franchise fee is usually due in one lump sum at the signing of the franchise agreement, but some franchisors allow franchisees to begin with a down payment and pay the rest in installments.

Royalty fees are due monthly, based on the previous month's gross sales. Paying on time pays off, as franchisors build a late fee into their agreements. If it's not in the agreement, try to negotiate a grace period of 10 days before this penalty is imposed.

Franchisors also ask for the right to audit your books. If the franchisor discovers that you've underreported gross sales, you'll pay for the audit in addition to unpaid royalties and other penalties. When reviewing the agreement, state that the amount underreported must be at least 1% to 2% of gross sales before you're penalized. That way, if you've made a small bookkeeping error, you won't be penalized unnecessarily.

Find out what happens if you default and terminate your agreement early. Some agreements give the franchisor the right to make you pay remaining royalties *for the entire term of the franchise*. If you're able to sell your franchise prior to defaulting, this won't be an issue. But if you can't sell and this provision is in your agreement, it could create a huge expense for you. Try to negotiate for the elimination of this provision if it exists, or at least have it reduced so there's a cap on the amount of time you'll have to pay royalties if you default.

Your Responsibilities and Obligations to the Franchisor

RESPONSIBILITIES AND OBLIGATIONS TO THE FRANCHISOR	SATISFIED	PROPOSED CHANGES
Do other franchisees have the same responsibilities and obligations that I have under this contract?		
Do I have to participate in the training program?		
Do I have to run the franchise myself or may I hire a manager?		
If I'm permitted to hire a manager, does the manager have to be a part-owner of the franchise?		
Are the operating hours and days spelled out in the contract or may I set my own operating hours?		
What accounting books and records must I show to the franchisor and how often?		
Am I responsible for making improvements or upgrades to the franchise site?		
Do I have to make additional improvements or upgrades at a specified time in the future?		
Is there a cap on the amount I have to spend now and in the future?		
Do I have to submit financial books to the franchisor? How often?		
Is there anything in the contract that guarantees uniform standards in the quality of the product or service?		
Are there provisions or penalties if those standards are not met?		
Will I have enough time to correct any deficiencies before I am in default of the agreement and terminated?		
Am I satisfied with the provisions of the non-compete clause if such a clause is included?		

Once you sign the franchise agreement, you are obligated to fulfill its terms. If your acquisition of the franchise is dependent upon your ability to obtain financing and find a good location, add this to the agreement. If you don't, and you can't get financing or find a location you and the franchisor agree on, you could lose everything you've already paid the franchisor. Another option is to put money into an escrow account until these contingencies are satisfied.

Non-Compete Clause

Most franchise agreements have "non-compete" clauses, which means you can't operate a competing business during the time of your franchise agreement, and usually for two or more years after the agreement expires.

For example, you may have built up a very successful pizza franchise, but after your franchise agreement ends, either you or your franchisor decides not to renew the agreement. You will then be prohibited from running another pizza establishment—and perhaps even any kind of food business—for a certain period of time. Obviously, this reduces your ability to succeed in another new business.

Try to have the non-compete clause removed entirely. If this is not possible, try to limit the amount of time and the scope of the non-compete. Another possibility is to have the clause removed in the event that you are willing to renew but the franchisor is not. Try to give yourself as many options as possible.

Personal Guarantee

Most franchisors make you sign a "personal guarantee" for all the obligations you make. Sometimes you can agree that this personal guarantee will only apply to the first two or three years of your franchise. If your spouse also signs, then your joint assets will be exposed, so avoid having your spouse sign if possible.

These are all issues that you want to carefully review with your experienced attorney. Only an experienced attorney can inform you of the long-term implications of these responsibilities and help you negotiate some of them more in your favor.

The Franchisor's Responsibilities and Obligations to You

FRANCHISOR'S RESPONSIBILITIES AND OBLIGATIONS	SATISFIED	PROPOSED CHANGES
What are the franchisor's contracted obligations to me on an ongoing basis?		
Will the training I get from the franchisor be sufficient?		
How many hours of training will there be? When will it happen?		
Do I have to travel to be trained?		
Will a trainer come to my franchise to assist with the opening?		
Do I have to pay extra for the training?		
If I have to travel to the training, do I have to pay travel and accommodation expenses?		
Are the operating hours and days spelled out in the contract or may I set my own operating hours?		
Will I receive ongoing training during the time I operate the franchise or just at the beginning?		
Will the franchisor provide advertising for my store or do I have to do my own?		
If the franchisor provides this advertising, do I have to pay extra for it (in addition to national or regional advertising)?		
If I am paying the franchisor for advertising, is the franchisor contractually obligated to use that money for local advertising? Or is the franchisor allowed to use it for national advertising that may not benefit me directly?		
If I'm doing my own advertising, does the franchisor have to pre-approve all advertising?		

Obtaining comprehensive and consistent support and services is essential to starting and building a successful franchise. Have your attorney examine the wording of the agreement closely. When it states that the franchisor *will* or *shall* do something, the franchisor is obligated to follow through. If the agreement says that the franchisor *may* or *might* do something (like help negotiate a lease), they aren't legally obligated to do so. Any such activity will be done only at their discretion.

Carefully review the terms according to which the franchise may be renewed, transferred, or terminated. All good things come to an end at some point, so think of your contract as an agreement that protects both sides when that time comes.

Franchise agreements commonly last for ten years. Negotiate an agreement that allows you to automatically renew if you want to. The renewal fee should be reasonable; it should not be another franchise fee. A $3,000 renewal fee is reasonable; a $30,000 renewal fee is not. Franchisors will make you sign a renewal according to the current terms, not according to the terms you signed 10 years earlier. But make sure that your basic agreements, such as royalty amounts and territorial rights, remain when you renew. These provisions need to be written into your new agreement.

If you are selling to a new (third-party) owner, try to negotiate your agreement so that the new owner acquires the existing franchise agreement for the duration of its term. Your franchise will be more appealing to a potential buyer if they can assume an existing agreement. If you sell your franchise to a new owner, a transfer fee averaging about $5,000 commonly applies. This covers the legal and administrative costs of approving the new franchisee.

Renewal, Transfer, and Termination Terms

RENEWAL, TRANSFER, AND TERMINATION TERMS	SATISFIED	PROPOSED CHANGES
When may my franchisor terminate my agreement?		
Are the reasons for termination listed in the franchise agreement?		
If my agreement may be terminated for breach of contract, does the agreement specify what constitutes breach of contract?		
May my contract be terminated if I don't produce what the franchisor considers to be enough income within a given period of time? If so, what is the required level of income?		
Do I have 30 days to correct a breach of contract before my franchisor can terminate?		
May I compete with this franchise if my agreement is terminated?		
If there is a non-compete clause in the agreement, how long does it last after the agreement expires?		
May I terminate the franchise agreement early if I want to?		
Is there a penalty or fee for doing that?		
May I transfer my franchise to someone else (such as heirs or family members)?		
If so, is there a transfer fee?		
What is the amount of the transfer fee?		
May I sell my franchise to a third party before the time of renewal?		
May I sell it to a family member or relative without the franchisor's approval?		
Will the transfer fee be lower if I sell to a family member?		
May I automatically renew my franchise so long as I have adequately performed my responsibilities?		
Will I have to make repairs or improvements or remodel with new décor as a condition of renewal?		
If so, is there a cap on the amount I will have to spend?		

Finalizing the agreement

At some point, negotiations will come to an end. You will not likely receive all the concessions you've requested. But your lawyer should be able to tell you what concessions are standard and which provisions are likely to be iron-clad.

After you've finished negotiating with the franchisor and have checked to ensure that everything in the franchise agreement is exactly what you've agreed to, you'll be sent the final franchise agreement to sign (or it may be given to you directly if you're at the franchisor's home office when the agreement has been reached).

You'll either pay the franchise fee when you sign the agreement or work out a franchise fee payment schedule. Then you'll begin the exciting process of starting up your franchise.

Do Your Homework

"*Call a cross-section of franchisees—big cities, small cities, high volume, low volume. What's their perspective of corporate? How do they treat people? Can you make money at this? What are the good and bad things about the franchise? Really pick their brains.*"

Chuck Griffin, BBB member and
owner of three Domino's Pizza restaurants,
Santa Cruz, California

Due Diligence

Interview Other Franchisees

The Big Dig

Burn up the phone lines and call people who are both current franchisees and those who have left the franchise. 'Why did you leave?' 'How do you like it?' 'Is the franchisor reasonable to deal with?' 'How's business?' 'Is it difficult to make the royalties?'

Peter Chase,
Franchise and Business Attorney,
Boston, Massachusetts

C arefully reviewing the UFOC is the first step in your due diligence—your investigation of the franchise you're considering. But documents can only tell you so much. For a truly realistic sense of what you're going to be getting, talk to others who've "been there, done that." After you and your lawyer have examined the UFOC, it's time to get on the phone and call and visit as many current and former franchisees as you can. You'll get a first-hand account of what to expect. And you'll get to know the franchisor better at the same time.

Throughout this process of due diligence, you'll also speak to representatives of the franchisor over the phone for a period of several weeks to several months. Even though the minimum cooling off period after receiving the UFOC is 10 days, you are likely—and well advised—to start the process immediately and take as much time as you need to complete your due diligence. When questions come up as a result of your discussions with other franchisees, raise them with your prospective franchisor. You'll get a better picture of the kind of people they are, what kind of business they run, and whether or not you can see yourself being in partnership with them.

Your job during due diligence is to find out as much as possible about the franchise you're considering. In this process you're looking to discover:

- What is the financial health of the franchisor?

- What are the backgrounds of the executives and managers who run the franchise?

- What will it be like to work with these people? Will they be there with the support you need to operate the franchise? Will you be able to work through disagreements in a fair and respectful manner?

- How long will it take me to turn a profit with this franchise? How much can I make?

- Does the franchise have a strong network of franchisees who support each other or a strong independent owners' association that represents franchisees' concerns to the franchisor?

- What work schedule and hours will be needed to make the franchise a success?

- How old is the franchise? How well established?

QUICK TIP

Temp Work

There's probably no better way to determine whether you and a franchise are a good fit than to work at the franchise you're interested in (in a managerial capacity), even if this is not mandated by the franchisor. Even if you work at a location for only a week or two, being part of their everyday routines can be a very quick and effective way to find out if you like the business.

QUICK TIP

Dialing for Advice

If the franchisor you're considering has an owners' association or a franchise advisory council, get the name and number of the head of the organization and of several additional members. These people will have a great overview of franchisor/franchisee relations. They can tell you about challenges the franchise is facing and how problems are solved within the system.

How to find them

Item 20 of the UFOC gives the names of franchisees and their contact information. This list includes current franchisees, as well as anyone who has left the company within the last year. You'll also be able to determine how many franchisees are in your area, your state, and the country. The listing also includes any company-owned outlets and the number of franchises the company expects to sell in the next year, which indicates how fast it is growing.

If there are only two or three names on the franchisee list, you're looking at a franchise that's either very young and untested or one for which there is simply not much of a market. Either way, you're taking a bigger risk if you go with such a franchise. There won't be enough franchisees to give you a good snapshot of the company—and you won't be getting one of franchising's biggest benefits: a proven business concept and operating system.

Talk to as many current and former franchisees as you can—at least a dozen. The number is limited only by your time and the time other franchisees are willing to give. Talk to franchisees from large and small markets, franchisees who are making lots of money, those who are losing money, and those who are just getting by. Make a point of visiting a franchisee in an area near the location where you're thinking of setting up or in a comparable market.

You'll find plenty of franchisors who have fair agreements and treat their franchisees well, but are their franchises automatically a good investment? Not necessarily. Sometimes, no matter how reputable the franchise, they are just not a good fit. One such example: A businessman planning to acquire a franchise in Los Angeles found a maid-service franchise that had happy franchisees and a fair franchise agreement. It had a strong training program, and the franchise fee was an affordable $45,000. There was only one problem: the cleaning service was located in the Midwest and all 20 franchises were in Kansas. No one on the West Coast had heard of the company. There was no brand-name recognition or marketing presence in Los Angeles. In this case, the franchise was not a good fit. Without the brand recognition and advertising presence, the franchisee would struggle to find a customer base.

What to ask

Not everyone you call will talk to you. Some will be too busy running their franchises, while others might view you as potential competition. But plenty of franchisees will be forthcoming and generous with their time. You may have to call two or three dozen to find 12 who'll take the time to talk to you. Tell them you're a prospective franchisee and ask for a convenient time to call back to interview them. Remember: They are extremely busy people, so be flexible about timing. They may only be able to talk at night after work or early in the morning. In some franchise systems, the franchisor will give you a code that you can pass on to franchisees so they know you're a legitimate caller. This can help open doors more quickly.

QUICK TIP

The Good, the Bad, and the Ugly

When interviewing franchisors and franchisees, don't be shy about asking tough questions. You need to know everything—the good, the bad, and the ugly—about the franchise. The more you know, the better you'll be able to choose the right fit.

Turn Up the Volume

"What you really want to investigate when researching franchises is: What kind of volume is this franchise going to do? Volume talks. The margins just aren't there unless you've got volume. Remember, as your volume increases, your fixed costs stay the same. Your lease, worker's comp, employee costs, and utilities all are basically the same. Plus, you sometimes get rebates or discounts on your supplies based on the volume you buy."

Chuck Griffin,
BBB member and owner of
three Domino's Pizza restaurants,
Santa Cruz, California

What are you looking for when you interview franchisees? Basically, you're trying to find out whether they're successful and satisfied in this franchise system and whether they'd recommend the franchise to you. Each time you talk to a franchisee, note whether that person is someone like you or someone looking for the same things in a franchise that you are. If people similar to you are doing well financially and happy with the franchisor, that's a positive sign.

Some franchisees won't answer all your questions. And not all the questions on the worksheets on pages 128-130 will be relevant to you. Focus on those that are the most important to your situation. Make copies of the worksheets or use a notebook to record additional information you receive from each franchisee. After you've done about half a dozen interviews, review your notes. You'll find you've probably received the same or similar answers to some of the questions. Other questions will have a range of answers. From this point on, focus more on the questions that still seem unsettled. If new questions arise, add them to your question list and speak to franchisees about them until you feel you have a complete picture of the franchise.

Don't limit your research solely to other franchisees. Talk to others who run similar non-franchised businesses in your area. Many of the ongoing expenses are similar for franchised and non-franchised businesses. Independent businesspeople can also tell you about industry trends, average costs for supplies and labor, and the kind of income you can expect. They can also give you perspective on the advantages and disadvantages of being independent versus being a member of a franchise in your industry.

If you're thinking of opening a sandwich franchise and know someone in your city who already operates a sandwich shop, call that person up and ask how big their shop is, how much they pay per square foot for rent, what sales volumes are, and how much they pay for payroll, supplies, and advertising expenses. How many sandwiches do they need to sell every week to turn a profit? Then call several franchisees from your franchise and ask the same questions.

When all your interviews are complete, take the basic information about costs and volume that you've obtained from franchisees and others in the same industry and apply it to your franchise.

Real Numbers

One of the things you'll want to learn during due diligence is how much it will cost you to start and operate your franchise. Putting real numbers on your business will tell you what it takes to get into the black. As you do your research with other franchisees, take the basic information about costs and volume you get from them and others in the same industry and apply it to your franchise.

For example, if you're thinking of going into a dry cleaning franchise, you'll start by talking to other owners in that franchise, as well as independent dry cleaner owners. Use what they tell you to estimate the size of the store you'll need (if you don't already have a location). If it's 1,800 square feet, estimate the average cost per square foot for commercial real estate in your area. Then add in the payroll for the employees you'll hire, cleaning supplies and other materials, utilities, and advertising. And don't forget your royalty payments.

Then figure out how many shirts and coats and other garments you'll need to clean per week to pay your expenses and generate a profit. How many items will you need to clean per week to generate X amount of sales, which is going to give you Y amount of profit?

This process will vary according to the franchise industry you're in. If you're going to be selling donuts, you need to figure your costs and then the number of donuts you'll need to sell to pay costs and generate the profit you want. How many of those will be sold with a coffee and how many without? Be specific when you figure out these numbers. If you're opening a hair salon or beauty franchise, estimate the average amount a customer will spend. If it's $30, how many appointments will you need to book every week to pay expenses and generate a profit?

If you go through this process, you'll see whether your proposed venture is workable in dollars and cents. Also look at total capacity. What's the maximum number of sandwiches you can make, shirts you can clean, or haircuts you can give? Is that capacity enough to pay the bills and make a profit?

Questions to Ask Franchisees

If you could do it over, would you buy this franchise again?

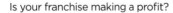

Is your franchise making a profit?

If so, how long did it take you to get in the black? What are your profit margins?

What kind of cash flow can I expect?

Is your franchise as profitable as you expected it to be when you bought it?

What kind of debt load are you carrying?

Did the franchisor provide you with good training? If so, how much?

Did the franchisor provide you with an operations manual?

Has the manual been helpful to you?

Is the franchisor easy to work with?

Is the franchisor demanding?

Is the franchisor honest and fair?

Does your franchise have a strong owners' association or advisory council? Has this association or council helped solve any problems the franchise has faced?

Were your startup costs accurately stated in the UFOC?

Are your ongoing costs accurately stated in the UFOC?

Are you reasonably satisfied with your franchise agreement?

Have you had any disputes with the franchisor?

If so, was your franchisor reasonable to deal with during the dispute?

Did you or the franchisor take legal action during the dispute?

Does the franchisor take the time to earnestly listen to your problems or concerns?

Do you know whether the franchisor has had problems with other franchisees?

Do you have relationships with other store owners? Is there a support network of store owners?

To your knowledge, has the franchisor had any legal problems?

Has the franchisor had any problems with competitors or government agencies in your area?

Are you happy with the advertising arrangement you have with the franchisor?

Are you happy with any marketing and promotional help the franchisor or has given you?

Do you feel your franchise product is unique enough that you have a niche?

Is the total investment described in the UFOC accurate compared to your total costs?

Do you buy inventory or services directly from the franchisor or specified suppliers?
Are you required to do so?

If so, are the prices fair and comparable to what other suppliers in the area charge?

Have you heard of any trouble with franchisees renewing or transferring their franchise?

Have you heard of any other franchises being terminated without good cause?

Are you satisfied with your relationship with your franchisor?

What was the most important help the franchisor gave you while you were starting up?

What do you wish the franchisor had provided but didn't?

Continued

How does the franchisor help you run your business on an ongoing basis?

What help would you like the franchisor to offer that they currently do not provide?

What is the best part about owning your franchise?

What do you like least about owning your franchise?

What are your average monthly sales?

How many employees do you have?

What is your labor cost?

What is your monthly cost for supplies?

How long have you owned this franchise?

How much do you bring home as income every year?

What would you most like to change in your franchise agreement if you could?

What disputes have you had with the franchisor? How did you settle them?

Are you satisfied with the renewal provisions of your contract?

Have you heard of franchisees who've had difficulty renewing their agreements?

Other:

Interview the Franchisor

A t the same time that you're calling other franchisees, you'll be engaging in an ongoing dialogue with the franchisor. After you send the franchisor some preliminary financial information about yourself to pre-qualify, the franchisor will send you the UFOC (and they'll often include the franchise agreement, as well). Review these documents carefully with an attorney, using the guidelines presented in Section 5 of this book.

Your main contact at the franchise will likely be somebody from the sales side of the company and will have a title like Franchise Sales Administrator, Director of New Franchise Development, or National Franchise Sales Coordinator. This person will gather your initial financial information, send you the UFOC, answer your questions, and help coordinate your discussions with the people in the various departments. Remember that this person is trying to sell you a franchise, but they are also trying to ascertain if you're a good fit for the franchise. It's helpful to develop a strong rapport with this person, because when you call or have a question, they'll be more likely to get back to you quickly. Establishing a good working relationship can be

QUICK TIP

Commissioned Answers

If you're speaking with a person from the sales department of a franchise, find out whether they're paid on commission. If they are, keep in mind that their job is to sell you the franchise—and take their information with an extra grain of salt.

instrumental in making sure your application gets the most serious consideration, especially for a highly competitive franchise.

You'll begin your due diligence with scheduled phone conversations (or if you live close to the franchisor's head-quarters, personal meetings) with representatives from the company. As you get more serious about each other, these meetings should eventually include executives and employ-ees from every department in the business—training, finance, operations, marketing, and customer service.

Smaller franchises won't necessarily have all these depart-ments but may have a person in charge of each function. If you have a training or finance question that can't be satis-factorily answered by a person from the sales or franchise development department, ask for a separate phone inter-view with the appropriate person.

In well-run franchises, while you are doing due diligence on the franchisor, the franchisor is checking you out, too. The franchise development personnel and salespeople know it hurts the franchise in the long term if there isn't a good fit between the franchisor and franchisee. A good franchisor will be most concerned with your potential for long-term success, not simply with getting your check for the franchise fee. How can you tell whether your franchisor is concerned with your success? Well-run franchises have a rigorous selec-tion process. They'll be honest with you about how much hard work it is to operate a franchise, and they'll encourage you to talk to as many other franchisees as you can. They'll make sure you're financially qualified for the entire cost of the franchise and able and willing to follow their system. They'll be clear and up front about what their expectations are and what services and support they'll provide.

The franchisor should welcome your questions, give straightforward answers, and not sugarcoat the financial burden or amount of work it will take to make your franchise a success. They should not be dismissive of your concerns, and they should take as much time as necessary to answer all your questions during the due diligence process. After all, if they're not willing to address the issues you raise now, they won't likely be very helpful once you become a franchisee.

As you interview the franchisor, ask yourself: Are these people I can trust and comfortably do business with? Will they listen to my concerns once I become a franchisee? Will they make decisions that will benefit the franchise system over the long term? Will I be able to go to them with a problem and be confident they'll help me solve it? Don't expect franchisors to solve all your problems for you. That's not their job. But the good ones will be there to help you when you reach a dead end on your own. The goal of interviewing is to learn whether you can count on them.

Discovery Day

After several weeks or months of discussions (likely over the phone and through email and regular mail), you may come to the conclusion that you're serious, and the franchisor may be convinced that you're more than a tire kicker. If you get to this point, the next step will be to visit company headquarters for a day-long "Discovery Day" to meet all the people you'll be working with if you do sign on. *A personal visit is absolutely essential.* Don't postpone your visit until just before you sign the contract. You are still doing due diligence at this point, not just shaking hands. Sometimes everything seems great over the phone, but when you meet in person, something just doesn't click. It's important that you get along well with the franchisor, trust them, and feel strongly that you can count on them.

On Discovery Day, make sure you meet various people, including senior executives, the heads of training, marketing, IT or technical, business or accounting, and customer service. In many franchise systems, the president or CEO of the company meets all prospective franchisees at this point, as well. Travel and accommodation costs are typically at your expense.

Site Visits

During your due diligence, it's a good idea to make personal visits to franchise outlets in your region. When you go into a store, you're usually looking at it from a consumer's point of view. But when you make these visits, look at the establishment from a business owner's viewpoint. Are there a lot of customers? Does the operation run smoothly and efficiently? Visit at different times of the day to see what the volume is like at different points in time. Do the employees and managers appear to have everything under control or are they overwhelmed? It's good to make anonymous visits, but it's also imperative to arrange visits with friendly franchisees who are willing to explain what you're seeing.

Considering the expense to you and the time for everyone involved, both sides must be quite serious by the time a personal visit to headquarters takes place. This is usually an all-day meeting, and it is most commonly after this face-to-face meeting that both sides decide whether or not to sign on the dotted line.

Throughout the due diligence process, take note of how you are treated by all the franchisor's personnel—not just the salesperson. If you don't feel that you're being treated well now, things won't get better once you've signed. At this point, when you are investigating becoming a franchisee, the franchisor will be treating you the best. Ask yourself these questions about the relationship the franchisor is developing with you. Do they take the time to meet with you? Do they thoughtfully listen and respond to your concerns? Do they seem to accurately and honestly disclose any challenges or problems? No franchise is perfect, so ask probing questions to reveal concerns other franchisees have had and how they've been addressed. Be skeptical of any franchise that tells you that 100% of franchisees are perfectly satisfied.

After Discovery Day, go home and reflect on your experience at headquarters and think over your impressions of those you've met before you sign any final agreements. A responsible franchise will not pressure you to sign immediately.

Questions to ask franchisors

The answers to the questions in the following worksheets will tell you what to expect from the franchisor, and they'll inform you about the franchisor's rights and responsibilities to you, as well as your rights and responsibilities to them.

Other questions will no doubt arise after your interviews with franchisees. Add these questions to the worksheet list, and make sure they're answered by the franchisor. Make copies of the worksheets or keep a notebook where you take notes on all your conversations with the franchisor, writing down the date and the name of the person you spoke with each time.

Remember: There are literally thousands of franchise opportunities available. If the answers to these questions leave you with more questions, there's no reason to go forward until you're totally satisfied with your choice. And if you're not satisfied with one franchise, you can move on to another available opportunity.

Questions for Franchisors

Will I be contractually guaranteed to be the only franchise in my territory for the length of the contract?

Can you sell other franchises in my market area?

If so, will I be offered the chance to buy the new franchise first? (This is called the right of first refusal.)

Do you retain the right to sell the company's product in supermarkets, chain stores, hospitals, or schools in my area—activities that could cut into my sales?

Do I have the right to use all logos, trademarks, and trade names associated with the franchise?

Do you allow sub-franchising? (A sub-franchisee acquires a franchise from a master franchisee, rather than from the franchisor.)

Will you provide me with the success and failure rates of your other franchises?

Will you give me the names and contact information for your most successful franchisees? Will you give me the names and contact information for your least successful franchisees?

Continued

Do I have to lease or sublet my space from you?

If not, will you help me find the best location for my franchise?

Do you provide financing?

Are your terms competitive with banks or other lenders in my area?

Do you charge any fees other than those you specified in the UFOC?

Will you give me information on actual sales and forecasted sales?

Will you provide me with information on actual profits or losses and projected profits or losses?

Will you provide numbers on actual profits and losses for specific franchises in your system?

If I am paying into an advertising fund, will that be used to promote my franchise specifically?

Are you currently in litigation with any of your franchisees?

Quick Tip

Look for Litigation

Some litigation against a successful franchise that has been around awhile is not unusual. But if there's a lot of litigation (a quarter or half of the franchisees have sued the company), that's cause for significant concern. And if a large number of franchisees are suing over the same issues, that's another red flag. One or two unrelated lawsuits, while they should be investigated, are not automatic cause for alarm. It's a good idea, however, to track down the people who are in litigation with the franchisor. After you talk to enough of them, a clearer picture of the franchisor will start to emerge.

Quick Tip

Google for Gripes

When you're looking for information about what life with a particular franchisor would be like, don't forget to enter the name of the company into a search engine and check for complaints. A simple search can uncover websites and message boards where current and former franchisees speak candidly about the types of challenges they encountered with the company and how these issues were—or were not—addressed. These sources can be invaluable in providing the kind of information you'd never get from company headquarters. You can also visit *www.bbb.org* to get BBB Reliability Reports to check for complaints and other vital data and statistics on the franchisor or, in some cases, the specific outlet, you're researching.

Additional questions for franchisors

The answers to the questions on the following pages will give you a better understanding of the franchisor's attitude and policy concerning transfers, renewals, and terminations. This will help clarify your obligations to the franchisor and the franchisor's obligations to you, as well as giving you a better idea of the amount of training and support you'll receive.

Add other questions to this list based on your interviews with other franchisees and personal visits to franchise outlets. You'll be talking to the franchisor repeatedly over the course of several weeks or months, so there's no need to have all your questions answered in one session. Just make sure they're all answered before you sign on the dotted line!

Additional Questions for Franchisors

What is the total investment you are requesting from me?

What do you do with the franchise fee? Is most of it reinvested in acquiring other franchisees or is a good portion used for training and support of existing franchisees?

Under what conditions can you terminate the franchise agreement early? Explain your termination process.

Explain your renewal process. What percentage of franchisees renew their agreement at the end of the first agreement?

Am I guaranteed an opportunity to renew?

How extensive is the training you will provide?

What skills or personality traits are frequently found among your highest-performing franchisees?

Have you had any bankruptcies in the past?

Are there any liens against your company?

What is your company's total amount of debt?

What is your company's total gross income?

What are your growth plans?

How many new franchisees do you add in a year?

What financial statements will you provide me with on an ongoing basis?

Am I required to buy inventory or services from you or a designated supplier? If so, please specify which goods and services and how much I will have to pay for them. Are these prices fair and comparable to what other suppliers in the area charge?

If I can buy inventory and services on my own, in what way do they have to meet your specifications or guidelines?

What marketing and promotional help will you provide for me on an ongoing basis?

What marketing and advertising am I required to do?

What exceptions or changes to the standard contract have you allowed other franchisees?

How big is your support staff? *(Most franchises have one support person for about every 10 franchisees. If you find a franchise that has a better ratio—say, 1 support person for every 7 or even 5 franchisees—that's good because you'll likely receive better and faster support.)*

Other:

What franchisors are looking for

A good number of franchisors will say that they are highly selective and make you feel that you'll be extremely fortunate to be "awarded" a franchise. This is true for the most popular, well-known brands, but for many franchisors, these words are more sales technique than reality. If you believe them, you may be tempted to present yourself in a way that will make them want to choose you. Remind yourself that your goal is also to discover whether you want to choose them. In the long run, you'll only win if you find a franchise that's a good fit for you—and that requires being honest with yourself and with the franchisor about who you are and what you're looking for.

The first thing a franchisor will want to do is make sure you're financially qualified. They usually check out your financial situation up front before they send you the UFOC, so by the time you go for the interview, that won't be a major issue.

Beyond that, what do franchisors want? If most franchisors were to describe their perfect candidate, it would be a former corporate executive who has a business background and has had experience managing people. This is a person who knows how to follow rules and operate within an established system but now wants to start working independently. An even more appealing candidate would be one with the above characteristics who has also already successfully owned and operated a different franchise.

But you don't have to be a former corporate executive or a former franchisee to do well as a franchisee or to be looked upon favorably by franchisors. These are just profiles of their dream candidates. Most franchisors are looking for outgoing, personable people. They're looking for people with business acumen, for people who are willing to work hard and who have a "fire in the belly," which means they'll do whatever is necessary to get a job done and succeed.

And they want people who will follow their system willingly and implement it successfully.

Good franchisors want to grow, but they want to grow with successful franchisees. Franchisors are constantly doing research to figure out why their most successful franchisees are successful and why the poor performers aren't doing well. They identify successful traits and then look for those traits in prospective franchisees. Most successful franchisors will tell you they have found this: The highest-performing franchisees are the ones who follow their system best. And that's why most of them are looking for new franchisees who they think will be very good at following their system.

Red Flags for Franchisors

The two biggest red flags for franchisors are a history of bankruptcies and you telling the franchisor that their franchise is too much work. Franchisors are looking for responsible businesspeople who'll put in the time to make the franchise successful.

Pre-Qualify Yourself

"*I talked to lenders before I put together my business plan. I told them my background and asked, 'Based on the cash I have available, if I find a franchise I'm qualified to do and put together a decent business plan, what kind of funds could I expect to borrow?'*

It's like pre-qualifying before you buy a house. I wanted to pre-qualify myself so when I talked to somebody I was interested in, I could talk to them seriously and know I could do the deal financially."

Maurice Dussaq, BBB member and
owner of two FastSigns Franchises,
Reno, Nevada

Finance *your* Franchise

Start-up Funding

S tarting any business takes money—a lot of it. And franchises are no exception. When you begin investigating the costs of starting a franchise, you'll first focus on the franchise fee. But the cost of launching a franchise business involves much more than just the franchise fee. You'll need to have money to fund all the usual expenses of a startup business, such as rent, location improvements, equipment, and inventory, and you'll then need enough working capital to run day-to-day operations until you become profitable. It's not unusual for franchisees to need $100,000 to $200,000 in startup money. The good news is that you don't have to provide all the startup investment in cash. Fortunately, there are many ways to finance your franchise.

The most common way to finance a franchise is to get a bank loan (or a loan from a savings bank or a credit union). Banks offer their own loans directly to business borrowers, and many banks also offer loans guaranteed by the Small Business Administration (SBA). If the franchise you're considering is registered with the Franchise Registry

QUICK TIP

Parallel Track

At the same time that you're in the process of selecting a franchise, you also have to investigate how to come up with the money to start your franchise. It takes a great deal of time—often many months—to obtain the financing you need. So don't wait until you've decided to sign on with a particular franchise to check out your financing options.

(*www.franchiseregistry.com*, a cooperative program of the SBA and FranData), your loan process will be streamlined.

Direct financing from franchisors is also becoming more prevalent, with more than 20% of franchises offering this option. Some franchises also have relationships with lending institutions to help their prospective franchisees obtain funding. You'll want to see whether the franchise you're considering offers any financing directly or can provide you with other financing assistance.

Another way to help fund your new franchise is to bring in a partner, investor, or group of investors. Such investors are called *equity investors*, because they get a percentage of ownership, or equity, in your business in return for their investment. If you go this route, you'll have to share any profits you earn, and most likely, share some of the decision making, as well. At the very least, you'll have to keep your partners or investors regularly informed about what is happening in the business.

Coming up with cash

Most financing sources expect you to make a substantial financial commitment to your own business. Even if they're confident of your abilities, they still want to see that you have your own money at stake. So expect to have to come up with at least part of the startup costs of launching a franchise. (The one exception is if you can find an investor who is willing to finance 100% of the business, which might be a relative or other investor who believes in you.)

In order to qualify for a loan, you'll usually be expected to provide 20% to 30% of the total amount of the loan or total startup costs (the amount may be as high as 50%, depending on the franchisor, lender, and your creditworthiness and assets). How will you come up with such a substantial amount of cash? The best source is likely to be your own savings. Other sources include the equity in your home or your retirement accounts.

Assessing Assets

We look at liquid assets. What's convertible to cash? Stocks are great, but when considering net worth, people will say I have 2 cars, my furniture, my flat-screen TV. Banks don't really care about that, and neither do we. We scrub down the financial statement to get a true net worth.

Michael Landry,
Franchise Sales Director,
Planet Beach Tanning and Day Spa,
New Orleans, Louisiana

Your Cash Contribution

The following chart outlines the pros and cons of various sources of the startup cash you'll be expected to contribute personally; in other words, the amount you'll have to contribute in addition to any loans or investments you receive from outside sources.

SOURCE	PROS	CONS
Personal savings	You've already got it. You don't have to pay anybody back or pay interest.	You may need that money for emergencies or for retirement.
Home equity loan or refinance your home	If you have substantial equity in your home, you can tap that for cash. For most people, their home is their biggest financial asset.	You'll be taking on new debt, and your monthly fixed expenses for your home will rise. Leave some equity in your home to access in case of emergency and to provide some peace of mind.
Credit cards	A quick source of money, especially if you have high credit limits. Little or no paperwork. May have some low "teaser" interest rates.	Credit cards are not designed for large, long-term debt. You'll pay high interest rates and substantial penalties for late payments. It's easy to incur large debt very quickly.
Sell stock, bonds, or other personal property	Like using personal savings, this means you don't have to pay anyone back or pay interest.	By liquidating other investments, you're putting all or most of your financial assets into one entity— your business.
Tap into pension, 401k, IRA, or other retirement accounts	You can legally tap into some retirement accounts to invest in your own business without penalties and taxes. Check with an attorney.	Once again, you're reducing your other assets, making you financially more vulnerable. You may be jeopardizing your retirement.
Funds from a relative or friend	If you have a willing friend or relative who believes in you, they may be willing to either invest in your business or loan you the cash. Make sure you put the terms of any agreement in writing, with the help of an attorney.	You may risk your relationship. Your friend or relative may start telling you how to run the business. You may feel guilty whenever you see them, especially if you can't pay the money back.
Take on a partner	A partner may come up with the cash needed to help you get other financing. The two of you may have an easier time qualifying for a loan together. The partner's talents could complement your skill set.	Partners get a share of the company's profits and, usually, a say in how the business is run.

No matter what source you choose, try to leave yourself some personal financial reserves. Every business is risky, and it's best if you don't have to put 100% of your net worth on the line.

Working Capital

The single biggest cause of franchise failure is undercapitalization—not having enough money to get the business off the ground and operating. Being stretched too thin during the startup phase of your business can make the difference between success and failure.

You'll need enough capital to open your doors, keep your franchise going during the startup phase until you're profitable (which could be a number of years), and cover your personal expenses.

Any loan you get should include working capital plus money to pay business bills and expenses until sales start covering expenses. It's common to include $30,000 to $50,000 in working capital. It's important to have this money not only so your business will make it through the first year, but also because most banks won't lend money unless they're convinced you have included enough capital in the loan to cover expenses until the business starts to pay for itself.

A benefit of being part of an established franchise system is that they'll share data on the typical costs of starting the business, not just the franchise fee, and this should give you a good idea of how much working capital you'll need until the business starts to make money.

Explore Your Financing Options

E ven if you have the cash to cover a substantial amount of the startup costs of a franchise yourself, it's likely that you'll need to finance a major part of your business. When financing a business, there are two basic choices—*debt* or *equity*.

With *debt* financing, you borrow money. In other words, you obtain a loan that you must pay back with interest. This increases your monthly overhead (since you usually have to make monthly loan payments) and increases the amount of long-term debt your company (or you) must pay back.

With *equity* financing, you get an investment. In other words, someone puts money into your business for a percentage of the ownership, or equity. You don't have to pay this money back, but you do have to share profits with the investor and you often have to share some of the decision making.

In either debt or equity financing, several options are available to you.

Banks

Most people turn to banks—or other lending institutions such as credit unions—for debt financing. After all, that's the business that banks are in: lending money. Banks are very interested in doing business, or *commercial*, lending, and you'll find them receptive to talking to you.

Banks may be particularly interested in working with you if you are acquiring a well-known franchise. After all, they'll feel there's less risk lending to a franchise within a well-established company with a recognized brand name and a proven operating system. Banks are also likely to have reviewed other loan applications for franchised businesses and will therefore probably be comfortable with the process.

Banks may also have a number of different loans available for you, including term loans, lines of credit, and one or more SBA-guaranteed loans (which are administered by banks, even though they are backed by the Small Business Administration).

Establish a relationship with a bank relatively early in your franchise selection process, as the loan process will likely take many weeks, even months. Once you have a fairly good grasp of the range of startup costs with different franchises, start searching for a bank. You'll want to get a good idea of how much money you're going to be able to borrow. This will help guide you in your choice of franchises.

When deciding on which bank to approach:

- Ask the franchisor if they have a relationship with any bank. If so, that bank will be very familiar with your specific franchise. That should make the loan process faster and easier.

- Ask other franchisees where they got their loans. Banks that have had positive experiences with other owners in your franchise system, or other franchisees in your industry, are likely to be more receptive to your application.

- Ask successful businesspeople in your town and your area which banks and bankers they recommend.

- Approach the banks you already have relationships with—for your personal banking, home loans, auto loans, savings, and so on.

Most bankers are receptive to the idea of franchises in general, recognizing that a good franchisor helps franchisees succeed. If you are seeking an SBA-guaranteed loan, the process will be speeded considerably if your franchise participates in the Franchise Registry (*www.franchiseregistry. com*). The Franchise Registry is a partnership between the SBA and FranData, designed to expedite the loan approval process for franchisees. (Even if your franchise is not listed, you may still be approved for an SBA-loan—although it will take longer.)

Your banker may be enthusiastic about the idea of franchises in general, and your franchise may be listed as part of the Franchise Registry, but your lender will still evaluate the viability of your franchise in your specific market. They want to make sure that the business makes solid business sense locally. That's why it's important to have a strong business plan, showing you've done your research into your market, competition, risks, and opportunities.

Potential lenders look at the viability of your business, but they'll also look at you as a person. They'll first be evaluating whether you appear capable of running the business successfully. They'll make that judgment based on personal meetings with you and on your employment and business background.

Most importantly, they'll want to know that you're the type of person who repays their debts and is capable of repaying the loan even if things don't go well with the business. They'll start by looking at your past credit record, and while it doesn't have to be perfect, be prepared to explain any past problems with your credit history.

INSIDER'S INSIGHT

Home Is Where the Money Is

We include home equity when we qualify franchisees. That's part of your net worth, and frankly, it's the largest asset you have. We recommend that if you've got that kind of equity, use it. If you get an SBA loan, the bank is going to attach the home anyway.

Roman Versch,
President and Owner
of Pet Depot franchise,
Los Angeles, California

How to Apply for a Loan

1. Take the numbers from Item 7 (Initial investment) of your UFOC. Then adjust those numbers to reflect the needs of your specific outlet and location. Using those numbers, determine the total amount you need to borrow. Include all the *startup costs* (franchise fee, legal fees, real estate build-out or purchase, supplies, inventory, training) and the *working capital* to pay bills until the business breaks even or shows a profit. As part of your working capital, include a draw or salary for yourself for at least six months to a year.

2. Identify various sources of financing. Comparison-shop before you choose a lender. Even if the franchisor offers financing or recommends preferred lenders, look around to see if the franchisor's terms are comparable with other lenders in your area. Interest rates and fees vary from lender to lender and often include loan origination fees, yearly maintenance fees, pre-payment penalty fees, and other costs. Find out the total cost of the loan, not just the interest rate.

3. Meet with each of your potential lenders. Before you meet, prepare a written loan proposal to leave with the lender. Ask the lender if they have standard application forms for you to fill out. To make the best impression, present your application forms, business plan, and other documents in a presentation folder, bound notebook, or three-ring binder.

Include in this proposal:

- Brief summary of your business and a table of contents for the material to follow

- Business plan (See pages 161-166 for more on how to prepare this.)

- Copy of franchise agreement

- Personal financial statement, which includes all your assets and liabilities and tax returns from the last three years

- At least two years of revenue and expense projections for the business

- Earnings claims provided by franchisor. If the franchisor doesn't provide earnings claims, use anonymous gross sales numbers provided in Item 19 (Earnings claims) of the UFOC.

- Audited financial statements from franchisor, showing company's balance sheets from past two years (Item 21 of UFOC)

- Letters of recommendation from local business leaders that attest to your business acumen, good character, responsible nature

4. Provide additional supporting documents as requested by lenders.

Depending on the size of the loan, the process can take several months. If you are working with an SBA-approved lender and your franchisor is included in the SBA/FranData Franchise Registry, the process will be streamlined.

Finally, lenders require collateral to guarantee repayment if your business doesn't create enough cash to do so. You'll be asked to sign a personal guarantee and use your home and other assets as collateral to cover the loan in case your business falters. So even if you didn't want to touch your home equity, your savings, or your stocks and bonds, expect to have to pledge them as collateral for your loan. That's the standard procedure.

Financing from the franchisor

Many franchisors offer some sort of financing to qualified franchisees. This happens either through direct financing by the franchisor to franchisees or through finance programs set up for the franchisee through third-party lenders. If your franchisor does offer financing, it will be described in Item 10 of their UFOC.

Each particular franchise system has specific applications, financing terms, and procedures. It may be easier to qualify and apply for these loans than for a traditional bank loan because the program is backed by the franchisor. However, these programs don't necessarily offer you the best terms or interest rates.

If your franchisor offers such a program, check it out. Are the terms comparable to what banks in your area offer? Compare their interest rates, their initial and ongoing fees, and the terms of the loan. For example, one of the loans may carry a pre-payment penalty and the other may not. One may require a large annual maintenance fee and the other won't. Compare all the fees and terms and then pick the program that offers you the best deal over the life of the loan.

Of course, if you are not able to qualify for a bank loan and the franchisor is willing to provide financing, this may be your only option. However, be cautious. Why are they willing to take a risk on you that others would not? Is it because they truly believe in you or because they are charging extremely high interest rates or because they are having trouble attracting franchisees and need to make it easy for potential operators?

Smaller, younger franchisors are more likely to offer loan assistance than more mature, established ones. The younger and smaller franchisors often don't have a long queue of people lining up to join (as some of the older, more popular franchisors do) and will go out of their way to facilitate financing.

Creative Financing from Franchisors

Some franchisors offer creative financing opportunities to help you get into business, and they are worth exploring. These can include:

- The franchisor becomes a co-investor with you in the business. In effect, your store becomes part company-owned outlet and part franchisee-owned outlet. Having a franchisor as a partner works in situations where you have insufficient funds to launch the business on your own, but the franchisor has great faith in your ability to operate the business and wants to partner with you.

- The franchisor defers payments on total startup costs until after you've been in business for a specified period of time. Part of the franchise fee may be deferred until after you've opened your location, or if you're getting financing directly from the franchisor, some of your payments may be deferred.

- The franchisor gets suppliers to finance the equipment you buy or helps finance these purchases itself. The franchisor is likely a volume buyer who sends a lot of business to these suppliers, so they may be able to get preferred rates.

- The franchisor acts as a guarantor of your loan from another lender. In effect, the franchisor takes the same role that the SBA takes when it guarantees loans.

- Franchisors often work with specific lenders who know their business well. They'll recommend you to these banks and lenders, who will be familiar with the franchise's business concept, and this will facilitate the loan process.

SBA Loans

Although you'll often hear the term *SBA loans*, the Small Business Administration doesn't actually lend money to businesses. Rather, the SBA guarantees, or backs, certain loans offered by banks and other lending institutions. In other words, if you default on the loan, the federal government pays the bank a certain amount of the loan.

Obviously, this guarantee lowers the risk to lenders and encourages them to loan money to small businesses they might not normally fund. Since new businesses are risky, banks are hesitant to make loans for brand-new ventures, including franchises. But with the SBA guarantee, they're more willing to take the risk.

Keep in mind that not all banks or lending institutions provide SBA-guaranteed loans. Check to see whether the banks you're considering do so. It is also possible that once you've been turned down for a regular loan from a bank, they will then consider offering you an SBA-backed loan.

The SBA expects many franchisees to apply for SBA-backed loans. In fact, it has set up a process to make it faster to obtain such loans. Franchisors can register with the Franchise Registry (*www. franchiseregistry.com*) by submitting their standard franchise agreement for approval. Even if the franchise you're considering is not yet in the Registry, you may still be eligible for an SBA-guaranteed loan.

Several different loan programs are available to franchisees through the SBA, including:

- **7(a) loans.** This program guarantees loans through SBA-approved lenders. It is the SBA's most widely used and flexible program. The loans can be used for working capital, equipment, machinery, building improvements, and refinancing other debt. The term of a loan is usually 10 years for working capital and up to 25 years for buildings and equipment.

- **CDC/504 loans.** These are designed specifically for real estate, such as hotel or restaurant construction, and are usually tied to job creation. The loans are long term (10 to 20 years) and fixed rate. They can be used to purchase real estate, machinery, or equipment, or to modernize or expand existing structures.

- **Microloan 7(m) loans.** These short-term loans provide up to $35,000 for working capital, inventory, supplies, furniture, fixtures, or equipment. They can't be used to buy real estate or to pay off existing debts. These are administered by nonprofit community agencies.

- **The SBA has special programs** for women entrepreneurs, veterans, Native Americans, minorities, and young entrepreneurs. You can explore these options online at *www.sba.gov/ services/specialaudiences*.

For a complete list of SBA programs, visit *www.sba. gov/services/financialassistance*.

Friends and family

You may be fortunate enough to have friends and family with the resources to provide some or all of the money you need—either as a loan or as an investment. These funds may be the easiest and fastest for you to *get,* but are they always the best type of money to *have?*

The advantages of getting money from friends and family are obvious:

■ You are already known to them, and they trust and believe in you.

■ You are likely to get the money faster than from other sources.

■ You may not have to disclose personal financial information you'd rather not share with a bank or investor.

■ You may receive a loan even if you have a spotty credit history.

■ If receiving a loan, you may have a relatively low interest rate (be careful to set a realistic interest rate or the Internal Revenue Service may treat this as a gift and tax it accordingly) and probably no other loan fees.

■ If receiving an investment, you may be able to negotiate a very good deal on the division of ownership.

But there are plenty of drawbacks to taking money from friends and family:

■ It may be very uncomfortable to approach a friend or family member.

■ You may have to disclose personal financial information you'd rather not share with people you know.

■ If they're investors, they'll have a say in decision making in your business and may second-guess your choices.

■ If they're investors, you may be tied to them for the life of your business.

- Even if they are lenders, they may be continually looking over your shoulder.

- They may have unrealistic expectations about the time it will take for you to pay them back or earn substantial profits.

- They may not be able to afford to lose the money if your business does not succeed.

If you do decide to turn to friends or family members for a loan or investment, keep in mind:

- Friends or family lenders should clearly understand the risks involved, the length of time it can take to pay them back, and the very real possibility that they could lose all their money.

- Put everything in writing and include a promissory note, signed by you, that details the amount of the loan, the interest rate, and the terms of repayment. This is *very* important.

- Put in writing what, if any, collateral you are pledging against a loan. Will your friend or family member get a lien against your home? Against any stocks or bonds or other financial assets? Against your car, boat, or other personal property?

- Detail—in writing—what type and level of participation your friend or family member will have in decision making in the company. How often will you report to them? Will they have the ability to make any decisions? If so, which ones? About what types of decisions will you consult with them?

- If this is an investment, have an experienced attorney help you develop the proper paperwork, delineating what percentage of ownership your investors are getting in the company and what rights they have. It is also a good idea to have an attorney draw up loan documents, as well.

QUICK TIP

Angel Investors

There's a huge amount of money available from angel investors for high-growth businesses. In 2005, over $23 billion was invested by these private investors. In addition to individual angel investors, virtually every community has an angel group. To learn more about how to find and attract money from angel investors, read *Finding an Angel Investor In A Day,* available at bookstores or at *www.planningshop.com.*

Private investors

You don't have to fund a franchise entirely on your own. You can bring in others to help finance your business. Many successful franchisees have partners or investors who've helped them launch their businesses.

A private investor can be someone you already know, such as a friend or family member, or it can be someone you find through networking in your community. It's even possible that the franchisor may know of individuals who want to invest in promising franchisees; perhaps other, successful franchisees, for instance, might want to invest in your location.

Angel investors are wealthy, private individuals who invest their own funds in high-growth ventures. Generally, they are most interested in startup technology or healthcare companies, but a franchise with a very successful track record or an exciting new franchise might be attractive to angel investors. A smaller, lesser-known franchise is far less likely to be attractive to angel investors.

Angel investors expect the entrepreneur—you—to be capable of running the business successfully. So they will look at your experience carefully, as well as evaluating the business opportunity itself. Angel investors will also expect you to contribute a portion of the funds yourself. Your investment may be as little as 10% to 20% of the cash, but angels like to see that the entrepreneur has their own "skin in the game," as well as building *sweat equity* by running the business.

Remember: When you take on an investor, they receive a portion of the ownership, or *equity,* in the company. You are now legally partners with them in the ownership—and the decision making—of the company. They will have certain rights and responsibilities, and these must be discussed in full with them (and put in writing in the financing documents).

Angel investors expect a fairly high *return on investment (ROI)* for their dollars (annualized out to about 30% to 40% per year), usually within a three- to five-year timeframe. Many successful franchises make enough money to enable the operator to live comfortably without generating the kinds of returns these investors require. If so, your franchise is not a good fit for an angel investor. Finally, remember that raising money from angel investors takes time. Expect it to take anywhere from a few months to a year.

Small Business Investment Companies (SBICs)

Another source of investment money for your business may be a Small Business Investment Company (SBIC). These are private investment firms that participate with the SBA in helping provide equity capital to promising small businesses.

Each SBIC is privately run and has its own investment criteria. Some invest only in certain industries or stages of development. Many will not be interested in franchise businesses. However, it may be worth checking to see whether an SBIC near you could be a source of investment capital for your business.

SBICs may provide equity (investment) funds only or a combination of investment and loans. As an investor, they will take an ownership interest in your business. Small

Business Investment Companies (SBICs) are licensed and regulated by the SBA. To find out more about this program, go to *www.sba.gov/services/financialassistance/equitycapital/investment*.

Other funding programs

Many people believe there's "free money from the government" for starting a business. That's not quite the case. There may be some highly targeted grants from federal agencies to achieve certain national goals (such as increasing exports), but generally, you won't be able to secure grants from government sources to help you finance your franchise. For a list of grants from U.S. federal funding sources, go to *www.sba.gov/services/financialassistance/grants/index.html*.

Some U.S. states and even large cities may have lower-interest loan programs. These are usually tied to job creation or manufacturing. There may even be some selected grants to help businesses start in economically challenged areas. To find a list of resources serving your area, check the Small Business Administration's website *www.sba.gov/localresources/index.html* or contact the Small Business Development Center (SBDC) serving your area (*www.asbdc-us.org*).

Remember: Regardless of what source you seek out to help you finance your franchise, raising money takes time, patience, and perseverance. Allow yourself many months for this process; don't wait until you've settled on a specific franchise before you begin your hunt for money. And don't get discouraged. You may have to knock on many doors before you find a willing funder.

Howdy, Partner

Taking on a partner can help make a franchise more affordable. This works best when the two partners have different areas of expertise. In an auto repair franchise, for example, one partner could be the mechanic and the other person would provide customer service and do advertising and accounting.

Partners can also be passive investors. A parent may want to provide seed money to a child to start their own business. Family, friends, and other partners can be a source of money, and they can put an otherwise unaffordable franchise within your reach.

Before you commit to a partner, however, consult with a good business attorney and get all the terms of your partnership agreement in writing. Some areas to consider:

- What each partner is responsible for

- Who has veto power over decisions

- How much time each partner will devote to the business

- What to do if a partner wants out ahead of plan

- How much each partner will put in to keep the business going

- What will happen if one partner dies and their portion of the business is inherited by a spouse or child

Write the Franchise Business Plan

Show Me the Money

Be realistic with yourself in putting a budget together, using knowledge from people who know about your kind of business. I've got a buddy who owns a sandwich shop and I know somebody who owns a Subway. I built a financial model and then I went to these guys and said, 'OK, what were your startup costs? What kind of rent do you guys pay? What are your insurance costs?' Then I talked to them and others about what I should expect from first-year sales. I was able to create my budget with real numbers from real people. I knew it might not be exact, but it was close enough to at least give me an idea of what kind of cash I was going to need for the first 12 months.

Todd Cameron, BBB member,
Subway franchise owner,
and venture capitalist,
Columbus, Ohio

S ome franchises may provide you with a sample or template business plan, but you will still need to develop a plan for your own location. Investors and lenders will require a business plan—not just a template from a franchisor—to see how well you've thought through your venture before they invest. They want to see that you grasp the issues and challenges of running the business and serving your market. Many franchises also require you to present a business plan before they'll accept you as a franchisee.

The information you'd include in a business plan for a franchise is similar to what you'd include in any business plan. However, there are specific issues that you should address in putting together a business plan for a franchise, including:

■ Indicators that the franchise will succeed in your market, regardless of how it performs nationally or in other markets

■ A thorough assessment of local competition—in your immediate vicinity and in the community as a whole

- An evaluation of the specific site chosen (for retail, food service, and other site-dependent businesses), the type of traffic patterns in that location, nearby competition, access, the specifics of your lease and build-out provisions

- What marketing and advertising you will do in your own market in addition to any national marketing done by the franchisor

- Specific issues of the franchise contract—such as limits on sourcing products, choice of products offered, pricing —and how they will affect the way you run your business

- Labor and personnel issues in your market and how they will affect your business in terms of labor costs and ability to find and keep employees

- Legal aspects of the franchise agreement that may affect your future, including renewal provisions

- Financial statements that reflect all fees, including ongoing franchise royalty fees, as well as initial franchise fees.

A well-developed business plan does more than just convince funders to provide the money you need to start your franchise. It does more than convince the franchisor that you've got what it takes to run a successful operation. The business planning process helps you make a positive impression on funders and franchisors. Once you've worked on your business plan, you'll be far more able to answer questions others ask you, proving to them that you are a thoughtful businessperson, who does your homework.

Quick Tip

Benefits of a Business Plan

You'll need a business plan to raise money, to prove to the franchisor that you understand your market, and most importantly, to succeed. The Planning Shop specializes in helping entrepreneurs develop successful business plans. *Business Plan In A Day*, and its accompanying Electronic Financial Worksheets, guides you through the entire process in a quick, clear, and easy fashion. Find it at bookstores or at *www.planningshop.com*.

Most importantly, a good business plan helps you figure out what it's going to take to succeed in your franchise in *your* location. It equips you to better understand and prepare for the real challenges you're likely to face. A good business plan enables you to better take advantage of the opportunities a good franchise in a good location can offer you.

A Franchise Business Plan

BUSINESS PLAN ELEMENT	WHAT IT IS	BE SURE TO INCLUDE
Executive summary	Provides a brief overview of your business and a short summary of the rest of your business plan. It's the most important part because it's the first (and sometimes only) part anyone reads.	Write it to be read by possible lenders, investors, landlords, leasing agents, and suppliers. Include amount you're seeking and what the money will be used for. Write it last—after you've worked out details of other sections. Should be 2–4 pages long.
Description of the franchise	Description of franchise, including company name and location, products, and services. Include number of outlets and a brief overview of franchisor's history.	Provide overview of industry, including changes or challenges. Describe franchisor's screening process and training program. Emphasize uniform quality of products and services offered.
Market analysis and strategy	Identify target customers, average age and income range, buying habits. Delineate the number of target customers in your market area, issues that impact the market in your area.	Include needs of potential customers and degree to which they are not being met. Explain why you believe you'll gain market share with your franchise.
Location analysis	Describe store location and why you chose the specific site. Include information about traffic, parking, and other businesses in the immediate area. This analysis should also include information about rent, length of lease, and renewal options.	Compare your site with other sites and explain why your chosen site is superior. Describe building (size, age, improvements) and signage near store that will drive customers to your location.
Competitive analysis	Identify current or upcoming competitors for products and services. Assess their strengths and weaknesses and any challenges you face in competing with them. If your franchise is a well-known brand, emphasize company's track record and reputation and market share and financial resources of franchisor.	Point to any weaknesses in the competition and strengths of your store and brand. Explain their weaknesses and why you will avoid problems they're having.

Continued

BUSINESS PLAN ELEMENT	WHAT IT IS	BE SURE TO INCLUDE
Management and staffing structure	Discuss key members of your management and staff and why each is qualified to manage operations, finance, accounting, personnel, and marketing. Describe personnel you'll need to hire and how you'll fill each position.	Focus on the backgrounds of members of management team. If you're the only person running the business, emphasize your skills and experience. Give names and backgrounds of advisors and business counselors you're using.
Day-to-day operations description	Explain your operating hours and products and services you'll provide. Describe staffing plans, training, and projected payroll. Include information about vendors and suppliers.	Emphasize proven operational structure mandated by franchisor and your ability to implement it.
Marketing plan	Describe franchisor's overall marketing strategy. Detail the local and neighborhood marketing that you will also do on a continuing basis.	Explain how you plan to launch your business and how you'll continue to attract customers. Include pricing and any promotional events you're planning.
Financing	State total startup investment you need for the franchise, as well as additional financing in the future. Provide profit and loss forecasts and cash-flow projections. Show amount of sales required to reach profitability and when this will occur.	Include franchise fee, equipment, lease and improvements, employee costs, supply and inventory costs, and working capital.
Contractual obligations	Include all important aspects of your franchise agreement. Detail franchise fees, royalties, marketing fees (if any), limits on supply sourcing. Specify the renewal provisions of your contract. Attach the franchise agreement.	Discuss training obligations, royalty and advertising fee structures, territorial protections, and renewal and termination terms. Include any comments from your attorney.
Strategy, implementation, and timetable	State projected opening date and how long you anticipate until the business breaks even and shows a profit. Define long-term goals and milestones.	Discuss risks in your venture. The more you show you anticipate and understand the risks, the better off you are.
Appendix	Supporting documents to strengthen your case. This includes financial statements, copies of tax returns, articles about your franchise company and the industry's growth potential, and a copy of the franchise agreement.	Include anything that shows you are likely to succeed.

Projecting your financials

A key part of your business plan is your financial projections. Every lender, investor, and franchisor and many landlords will want to see your financials. So these are very important. Moreover, as a business owner, it's time to become comfortable with key financial documents. The three most important financial documents are:

- The Income Statement

- Cash-Flow Statement

- Balance Sheet

Standard financial forms may not include key costs for franchisees, such as your up-front franchise fee and your ongoing monthly royalty fees. So you'll have to adjust any financial templates to include these key costs. Remember: The monthly royalty fees that you'll pay the franchisor are typically paid on your *gross income,* or the total dollars you take in before any expenses. In other words, that cost comes "off the top." So be certain your financial documents reflect those fees accurately. They'll have a major impact on your total profitability and cash flow.

Financial projections are just that—informed projections of what your financial condition will look like at a future date, based on realistic estimates of income, expenses, market growth, and such. Your financial projections must look professional and be realistic, but they aren't going to be right on the mark. In fact, it's impossible to project your financial future perfectly. But your financials do provide a benchmark for future performance and give lenders and investors an idea of what to expect.

- **Income Statement,** also known as your Profit and Loss Statement, or P&L, summarizes the income and expenses of your business and shows whether or not the business, as a whole, is profitable. It shows how much money a company is earning or losing over a specific period of time.

- **Cash-Flow Statement** shows the cash position of the company. A company may be profitable but still not have cash in the bank to pay the bills, due to the timing of income and expenses. The cash-flow statement shows the money coming in and going out of a company.

- **Balance Sheet** indicates the total value of the company, based on its assets and liabilities. The balance sheet reflects both long-term liabilities, such as loans, and short-term liabilities, such as Accounts Payable, as well as the value of fixed assets, such as equipment, and Accounts Receivable.

Welcome to the World of Franchise Ownership

A cquiring a franchise can be a route to financial independence, being your own boss, doing work you love, and gaining the substantial pride that comes from building a new business and creating jobs in your community. Franchising is a proven method of helping would-be entrepreneurs build successful businesses. For nearly a century, franchising has worked to serve the needs of both the franchisor and individual would-be business owners. The franchisor receives the benefit of a highly motivated partner (and their financial commitment) to help expand their business quickly. The franchisee acquires a proven product with a built-in business system and a recognized brand name. In the best franchises, everyone wins.

As a result, the number and types of franchises have expanded rapidly, and the range of industries offering franchise opportunities is now almost unlimited. In fact, if you are the type of person who will thrive operating a franchised business, there's most likely one out there that will work for you.

But every franchise is different. Costs vary widely. Contracts, fees, obligations, and rights vary widely. And the capabilities, personalities, and business ethics of those who run specific franchises also vary.

Since acquiring a franchise is likely to be the biggest expense you'll ever have—often rivaling the cost of a home—you must take the time to explore your options diligently before taking on the obligations of running a franchise.

In this book, you've explored the steps to follow in researching and evaluating franchises —and yourself. These included:

- Choose a franchise that meets your personal goals and situation
- Choose a franchise that will succeed in *your* market
- Carefully examine and investigate the franchises you're considering
- Thoroughly read and understand the UFOC and the franchise agreement
- Work with an experienced franchise attorney to understand your rights and obligations and the franchisors' rights and obligations in relation to you
- Understand the very real financial and time commitments of your specific franchise
- Evaluate whether the franchise supplies you with the support, training, and business structure you need
- Seriously reflect on whether you will be comfortable with the obligations and limitations the franchisor places on you
- Evaluate your financial resources and potential funding sources

- Choose a franchise that is well within your financial resources

- Secure the funding you need for both startup expenses and ongoing working capital for at least a year

- Find a funding source that offers a reasonable and fair deal, in terms of interest rates and fees or equity distribution

During the course of this investigation, you may have discovered that operating within a franchise environment doesn't work for you. You may not be comfortable running your own business within the limitations placed on you by any franchisor. You may decide that you'd be happier running your own independent business or that running a business just isn't for you. If so, your time has been well spent. It's much better to find out that franchised businesses aren't for you before you invest your money and many years of your life.

On the other hand, you may have realized that you do, indeed, prefer the structure and benefits offered by a franchised business opportunity. Ideally, this book has helped you to find the right franchise for you—one that fits your personality, working style, goals, and financial situation. Make certain that you've selected a franchise that is operated honestly and ethically, that has good relations with its current franchisees, and that is committed to your long-term success.

With a franchise, as with any business, there are risks—but there are also opportunities. Drive down almost any major business street and you'll see successful franchises. Flip through a business phone directory and you'll find many franchised services. Franchising works—and it can work for you, too. Good luck with your new business!

The Best Policy

"I've been on both sides. I've been a franchisor making the final decision on selecting franchisees, and I've been a prospective franchisee. If you're smart, you look at it the same way you do a job interview. Go in and present yourself in the best light you can. But be honest, because if you're not, it will be to your own detriment."

Maurice Dussaq, BBB Executive Committee
and Board of Directors member and
owner of two FastSigns franchises,
Reno, Nevada

Resources

Resources

M any organizations, websites, books, magazines, and conferences exist to help you research and acquire a franchise. The main sources are included here. They're constantly changing and evolving, so check the websites for the most current information.

To research potential franchises and any complaints about them

Better Business Bureau

4200 Wilson Blvd, Suite 800
Arlington, VA 22203-1838
703-276-0100
www.bbb.com

The Better Business Bureau provides information on nearly 3 million businesses and organizations. You can find out whether the company you're investigating is a BBB member or if any complaints have been filed against the company. If you're unsure where the nearest BBB is located, go to the BBB home page and click on "Locate a Bureau."

Franchise trade organizations

American Association of Franchisees and Dealers

P.O. Box 81887
San Diego, CA 92138-1887
1-800-733-9858
619-209-3775
www.aafd.org

The AAFD focuses on creating fairness standards for franchisees. It created the franchisee "Bill of Rights." It developed fair franchising standards and gives a "fair franchising seal" of approval to franchisors who conform to these standards.

The organization supports independent franchisee associations, which give franchisees an effective voice in their franchises. In addition to being a source for research into individual franchises, the AAFD provides information on legal or financial advisors and the marketplace.

American Franchisee Association

53 West Jackson Boulevard, Suite 1157
Chicago, Illinois 60604
312-431-0545
www.franchisee.org

A franchisee-rights organization, this trade group also has a database of franchise attorneys and offers help in evaluating franchise agreements and UFOCs.

International Franchise Association

1501 K Street, N.W. Suite 350
Washington, D.C. 20005
202-628-8000
www.franchise.org

IFA is the largest trade organization for franchising. Sections of its site are devoted to finding the right franchise, using your 401k to acquire a franchise, the FTC *Consumer Guide to Buying a Franchise* and *Franchising for Veterans*. Over 1,000 franchises for sale are listed on the site, and there are referrals for franchise attorneys and accountants. You can also find educational opportunities, including seminars and conferences.

Franchise research and analysis

FranData

1655 N. Fort Myer Drive, Suite 410
Arlington, VA 22209
703-740-4700
1-800-485-9570
www.frandata.com

FranData compiles exhaustive research on overall franchising trends, but also does custom research, including individual market research or sector and competitor analysis.

FranSurvey

P.O. Box 6385
Lincoln, Nebraska
68506-0385
1-800-410-5205
www.fransurvey.com

FranSurvey does some of your homework for you by calling all franchisees from a franchise and asking them 20 key questions (including, "Knowing what you know now, and if you had it to do all over again, how likely would you be to buy this franchise?"). The site claims to get responses from 75% of the franchisees they contact. They provide the responses in a report and grant "World Class Franchise" status to franchisors who get glowing reviews from their franchisees. This information can be useful to supplement your own research but should not substitute for calling some franchisees yourself to get first-person information.

U.S. Census

www.census.gov
http://quickfacts.census.gov

These government sites can help with market research and provide data (population density, average age, average income, and more) on your area of interest. Even though national census data is updated only every 10 years, the U.S. Census provides many annual surveys, including surveys of manufacturers, geographic area statistics, value of product shipments, and statistics for various industries and industry groups.

Help from experienced businesspeople

Federal Trade Commission (FTC)

600 Pennsylvania Ave., NW
Washington, D.C. 20580
202-326-2222
www.ftc.gov

In addition to regulating the franchise industry, the FTC offers a *Consumer Guide to Buying a Franchise*. This document gives general advice on how to research and evaluate various franchises. However, it doesn't list particular franchises for sale, nor does it rate the quality of any particular franchise. The FTC's website also provides consumer protection information on franchise and business opportunities.

The Planning Shop

555 Bryant Street #180
Palo Alto, CA 94301
650-289-9120
www.PlanningShop.com

The Planning Shop publishes many books on how to start and run your own business and how to write a successful business plan. Among it bestselling titles are *Business Plan In A Day, Angel Investor In A Day,* and *The Successful Business Plan: Secrets and Strategies.*

Service Corps of Retired Executives (SCORE)

SCORE Association
409 3rd Street, SW, 6th Floor
Washington, DC 20024
1-800-634-0245
www.score.org

SCORE calls itself "Counselors to America's Small Business." It's a nonprofit organization founded in 1964 to help small businesses flourish by offering business advice and training. They're dedicated to helping educate aspiring entrepreneurs in the formation, growth, and success of their businesses.

SCORE is oriented to the real world. It uses over 10,000 volunteers who share the wisdom and lessons learned from their own businesses. The volunteers are working or retired business owners, executives, and corporate leaders.

Small Business Development Centers

Association of Small Business Development Centers
8990 Burke Lake Road
Burke, Virginia 22015
703-764-9850
www.asbdc-us.org

Small Business Development Centers offer *free* counseling and seminars for small business entrepreneurs across the country. These are usually held on a college or university campus and taught by college professors and usually include a lot of information about starting a franchise. The SBDC delivers up-to-date counseling, training, and technical assistance in all aspects of small business management. The program was established in 1980, and SBDCs are funded by state and local partnerships, matched by funds from the SBA. There are now over 1,100 local SBDC offices.

You'll find help with legal, financial, marketing, and technical problems, as well as information on federal, state, and local assistance programs. The SBDC is a great resource for future and current franchisees, providing assistance and classes in everything from finding the right franchise to financing your franchise.

You can also access the SBDC through the Small Business Administration (SBA).

SBA Answer Desk

6302 Fairview Road, Suite 300
Charlotte, North Carolina 28210
1-800-827-5722
www.sbaonline.sba.gov/sbdc/

Go to the website and click on the SBDC Locator on the home page to find the office nearest you.

Special SBDC programs and economic development activities include international trade assistance, technical assistance, procurement assistance, venture capital formation, and rural development. SBDC makes special efforts to reach minority members of socially and economically disadvantaged groups, veterans, women, and the disabled. Assistance is provided to both current and potential small business owners. SBDC also provides assistance to small businesses applying for Small Business Innovation and Research (SBIR) grants from federal agencies.

The SBA's Franchise Registry

www.franchiseregistry.com

The Small Business Administration (SBA) has already reviewed the franchise agreements of franchises listed in the Franchise Registry, and that means franchisees get a streamlined review process when applying for SBA loans.

Websites

Many websites are devoted to franchising. New ones crop up from time to time, and changes are made to existing ones frequently. Among the most trafficked sites:

- *www.americasbestfranchises.com* offers a franchise directory and resources to help you find financing for your franchise. Franchise directory listings are presented by franchisors, but the website also has links to FranSurvey, which interviews franchisees from various franchises, in order to rate franchisors.

- *www.business.gov* is a U.S. government website that provides good general information about acquiring a franchise.

- *www.franchisegator.com* has a franchise directory with frequent updates on available franchises, feature articles on financing, and listings of upcoming franchise conferences. The directory presents franchisors' descriptions but does not critically compare various franchises.

- *www.franchisehandbook.com* or *www.franchise1.com* produces the quarterly *Franchise Handbook*, a directory of 1,700 franchises in 65 categories. It also has an online database of franchises, franchise consultants, and franchise conferences.

- *www.franchisehelp.com* has a franchise directory and fee-based research and reports, including industry surveys and reports on various franchise sectors and companies. UFOCs are available for purchase, and there are special sections for potential franchisees, including help with franchise selection.

- *www.franchisesolutions.com* has a franchise directory, news and advice columns, and special sections for women and veterans. The articles tend to be industry fluff pieces.

- *www.franmarket.com* has information on financing, startup strategies, marketing, and other issues for franchisees, as well as a directory of franchises available worldwide. The website is produced in conjunction with SCORE, the Service Corps of Retired Executives.

- *www.nase.com* is the National Association for the Self-Employed and calls itself "The Nation's Leading Resource for Micro Businesses." It provides a lot of information on starting and running a business and offers group health insurance, a great benefit for franchisees.

- *www.startupjournal.com* is published online by the *Wall Street Journal* and is aimed at budding entrepreneurs. It has a section devoted to franchising and a section listing franchises for sale. Articles include "Franchisee Knows Value of Good Employees" and "First-Time Franchisees Face Tougher Road."

- *www.worldfranchising.com* lists Bond's 100 Top Franchises and Bond's 50 Under 50 Franchises—50 up-and-coming franchises with under 50 units. The site also includes links to its sister websites to help you find a franchise attorney or franchise consultant. Included on this site is a section listing franchisors dedicated to increasing representation by members of minority communities.

Print directories

Print directories of franchises offer a wealth of information. Some are updated quarterly, but most have annual updates. Check directory websites to order the most current version. The following are among the most useful directories.

- *Bond's Franchise Guide*. An annual guide with detailed profiles of over 1,000 franchisors in 45 business categories. Cost: $29.95. Available from *www.sourcebookpublications.com* or from *www.worldfranchising.com,* at the Franchise Bookstore.

- *Bond's Top 100 Franchises*. An annual list of top franchises in the food-service, retail, and service-based industries. Companies are evaluated on many factors, including franchisee satisfaction, level of initial training and ongoing support, market dynamics, and financial stability. Cost: $19.95. Available from *www.sourcebookpublications.com* or from *www.worldfranchising.com* at the Franchise Bookstore.

■ *The Franchise Handbook.* A directory of 1,700 franchises in 65 categories, updated quarterly. Each listing has a description of the franchise, address, contact, and phone number, as well as franchise fee, total initial capital investment, number of franchises, type of training offered, and other information. Cost: $6.99 per issue or $22.95 for 4 issues. Available at *www.franchisehandbook.com.*

■ *The Franchise Opportunities Guide.* Published by the International Franchise Association twice a year. This franchise directory offers brief company description, initial investment required, training provided, and contact information. Cost: $17.00. Call 1-800-543-1038 or go to *www.franchise.org* for more information.

■ *Franchise Times' Super Book of Franchise Opportunities.* This large franchise directory offers complete descriptions, contact information, and investment profiles. It will be updated regularly on the Franchise Times website. Available at *www.franchisetimes.com.*

■ *Franchise Update Publications.* This company offers several guides, including *The Executive's Guide to Franchise Opportunities*, *Food Service Guide to Franchise Opportunities*, and *The Guide to Multiple-Unit Franchise Opportunities*. Available at *www.franchise-update.com.*

■ *How Much Can I Make?* This book details the earnings claims of 112 different franchise operations. The information is provided by the franchisors through their Earnings Claims Statements. This data provides a starting point only for helping you figure out how much you might make in a similar business. Cost: $29.95. Available from *www.sourcebookpublications.com* or from *www.worldfranchising.com,* at the Franchise Bookstore.

■ *Minority Franchise Guide.* This directory has profiles of almost 500 companies that encourage and support minority franchisees. Cost: $19.95. Available from *www.sourcebookpublications.com* or from *www.worldfranchising.com,* at the Franchise Bookstore.

Trade shows, conferences, and seminars

Trade shows are a great way to be introduced to multiple franchises in a short amount of time. Numerous conferences and trade shows are held coast to coast year round. These shows include educational forums that give you the opportunity to meet representatives of many franchises in person. Some shows combine franchises with other business opportunities.

Franchisors hand out promotional brochures at these events, and some also hold mini-seminars on their franchise and even give out their UFOC to people they consider serious candidates. To be considered a serious candidate, you have to fill out a financial profile to pre-qualify. You can find current conference schedules on most of the websites listed below.

You can't actually buy a franchise at a trade show. Even if a franchisor gives you the UFOC, there is a legally required 10-day "cooling off" period between the time when you receive the UFOC and the point at which you sign a franchise agreement. So if a company says they can sign you up that day at a trade show, it's not a franchise.

The U.S. Small Business Administration (SBA) sponsors seminars in many communities through Small Business Development Centers (SBDCs). Search on the Internet for SBDCs in your community, which are often located on college campuses. Taught by college professors, these seminars sometimes include information about starting a franchise.

Some of the bigger trade shows and conferences include:

■ **AAFD Annual Conference.** The conference of the American Association of Franchisees and Dealers (AAFD) focuses on building fair franchising standards and improving franchisee associations but also has franchise exhibitors, networking opportunities with other franchisees and suppliers, and free consultations with business experts. It's more for existing franchisees but could also be useful if you're on the verge of acquiring a franchise. Cost: $375–$425. Go to *www.aafd.org* for more information.

- **Franchise and Business Opportunity Conferences.** This traveling show takes place almost every month in various cities throughout the U.S. and Canada. It brings buyers and sellers together, providing opportunities to meet franchisors (or their sales reps) in person to find out more about various franchises. Seminars are also offered on topics such as financing a franchise or leasing. Admission is generally $10. For information, call 1-800-891-4859 or go to *www.franchiseshowinfo.com.*

- **Franchise Expo South.** This show serves the southeastern U.S., Latin America, and the Caribbean. Along with a conference program, the three-day event brings franchisors together with potential franchisees. Basic admission is $15 per day, and there are extra fees for some symposiums. Go to *www.franchiseexposouth.com* for more information.

- **IFA Annual Convention.** The International Franchise Association's annual convention is a massive, four-day event with general and break-out sessions covering everything from effective communication between franchisors and franchisees to effective marketing techniques. This convention is geared more toward franchisors than franchisees, but there's plenty for franchisees, as well. There are keynotes by industry luminaries, an exhibitor hall, and lots of networking opportunities. Admission, including conference and seminars, is $899. Go to *www.franchise.org* for more information.

- **International Franchise Expo.** Sponsored by the International Franchise Association, this annual event showcases hundreds of franchise concepts, attracting franchisors, investors, and potential franchisees from throughout the U.S. and 80 other countries. The three-day event also has a conference program. For more information, go to *www.franchiseexpo.com.*

- **Multiunit Franchising Development Conference & Expo.** Organized by Franchise Update, this conference is for franchisees interested in becoming multi-unit operators and brings together franchisors, franchisees, suppliers, and investors. Go to *www.areadeveloper.us/mudco/* or *www.franchise-update.com* for more information.

- **West Coast Franchise Expo.** This is an annual, three-day event sponsored by the International Franchise Association, aimed at potential franchisees from over a dozen states in the West. It showcases over two hundred franchise concepts, representing a wide variety of industries at all investment levels. In addition to the exposition, a full conference program and numerous seminars are offered. Go to *www.wcfexpo.com* for more information.

A variety of other franchise trade shows takes place across the U.S. Some of these are sponsored by a single franchisor with multiple brands. For example, Raving Brands (*www.ravingbrands.com*) is a company with nine different franchise brands under one corporate umbrella. It takes its "tour days" to various cities across the country to sell franchises and usually meets in airport hotels. These types of shows can be helpful for gathering information about particular brands, but they are limited to the offerings of the one parent company.

Magazines

Several magazines regularly cover the franchise industry, and they're full of advertisements for franchising opportunities. Look in the backs of the magazines for the ads.

- *Entrepreneur.* Monthly magazine for the small business-person. Covers franchising consistently. The magazine rates franchises and has an annual "Franchise 500," the 500 top franchises selected by the editors of the magazine. Subscription is $16 per year through *www.entrepreneur.com* or call 1-800-274-6229. Single issues also available on newsstands.

- *Franchise Market Magazine.* Published quarterly in cooperation with SCORE (Service Corps of Retired Executives) and distributed in 389 SCORE offices nationwide. Also available online at the website. It has features like "10 Dumb Things to Avoid When Buying a Business." It also includes the Top 100 New Franchises started since 2000. Go to *www.franmarket.com* for more information.

- *Franchise Times.* News and features covering the franchise industry, aimed at franchisees and franchisors alike. Lots of information available on franchise financing and opportunities to acquire a franchise. Subscription is $35 per year. Call 1-800-528-3296 or go to *www.franchisetimes.com.*

- *Franchise Update.* Geared more toward franchisors than franchisees, this quarterly magazine has listings of franchises for sale. Subscription is $40 per year. For more information go to *www.franchise-update.com.*

- *Franchising World.* Published monthly. The official magazine of the International Franchise Association (IFA). Subscription is $50 per year. Call 1-800-543-1038 or visit *www.franchise.org.*

- *Inc.* Magazine aimed at the small business entrepreneur. Its website has a franchise directory. Special features and how-to guides on acquiring a franchise, financing, raising capital, and finding a mentor. Online subscription rate is $10 per year. Go to *www.inc.com* for more information. Single issues also available on newsstands.

Glossary
of Common Franchise Terms

Advertising Fee: A fee paid for developing advertising and marketing for the franchise system. The advertising fee is often a percentage of gross sales, but franchises vary widely in how they use this fee, and some franchisors do no advertising and charge no fee. The fee generally covers national and regional advertising, but not necessarily local. The specific advertising of individual locations is still usually the responsibility of the franchisee.

Area Developer: A franchisee who purchases the exclusive right to build multiple franchise units in a specified territory.

Business-Format Franchise: A franchise where the franchisee acquires the right to use a brand name and trademark for a specific length of time and to distribute the products and/or services of the franchise that owns the brand name and trademark. In this type of franchise, the franchisees also use the business and operating system provided by the franchise to run their local businesses. This is the type of franchise discussed throughout this book. It is different from a product franchise, where the most important thing the franchisee receives is the product the manufacturer makes, not the business and operational system.

Co-Branding: Offering two or more different franchise brands side by side or under the same roof. Taco Bell and Kentucky Fried Chicken outlets are co-branded when they're at the same location.

Company-owned outlet: Some franchises own and operate some of their stores themselves. These are the company-owned outlets, which exist in addition to the stores franchisors license to franchisees to operate.

Conversion Franchisee: An independent small businessperson who joins a franchise system and changes the name of their business to that of the franchise. The conversion franchisee also takes on the operational system of the franchise. Joe's Sandwich Shop could become Subway, for example.

Exclusive Territory: A defined area in which only one franchisee has the right to sell the franchise's products and services. Negotiables in this type of arrangement include the extent of the territory and whether or not the franchisee has exclusive rights to it. The results of the negotiations are stated in the franchise agreement.

Federal Trade Commission (FTC): The federal agency of the U.S. government that regulates the disclosure rules and selling processes of franchises. The FTC initiated the format for the franchise disclosure document, the Uniform Franchise Offering Circular (UFOC).

Franchise Agreement: This is the legal document, signed by both the franchisor and the franchisee, that contains all the obligations and responsibilities of each party. It differs from the UFOC, which is a disclosure document that gives general information about the franchisor and obligations of the franchisee. The franchise agreement is a binding contract; the UFOC is an information document only.

Franchise Fee: The initial, up-front fee paid for the right to use a company's brand name, trademark, and business and operating systems for a specified amount of time. The fee usually includes some training and assistance.

Franchisee: A person who acquires a franchise is a franchisee.

Franchisor: The company that sells the right to use its name and operating system is the franchisor.

Initial Investment: The amount of money needed to acquire a franchise and keep it running during an initial start-up period—usually three months. It includes the franchise fee, equipment, initial supply and inventory, the lease and leasehold improvements, deposits, fees, licenses, and professional costs, and the working capital required during start-up.

Master Franchisee: A franchisee who has acquired exclusive rights to build several units in a specified area. Unlike the Area Developer, the Master Franchisee doesn't develop the units, but sells them to other franchisees instead.

Ongoing Support: After the initial training, the help that the franchisor gives to up-and-running franchises. This includes ongoing training; help with problem solving; and the introduction of new operations, procedures, products, or services.

Registration States: The 15 states that have rules and regulations, in addition to the federal FTC regulations, governing the disclosure and sale of franchises within each of those states.

Renewal Fee: Once the original term of a franchise is completed, if the franchisor and franchisee agree on a new term, the franchisee pays this renewal fee to the franchisor.

Right of First Refusal: If franchisees wish to sell their franchises, this gives the franchisor the right to match any legitimate offer the franchisee receives, thereby acquiring the franchise itself.

Royalty Fees: Monthly payments that the franchisee makes to the franchisor for the life of the franchise agreement. These are usually a percentage of gross sales receipts, but they are sometimes a flat fee.

Sub-franchisee: When a franchisee acquires a franchise from a master franchisee instead of from the franchisor, he or she becomes a sub-franchisee. The sub-franchisee often receives training, support, and supplies from the master franchisee, who is usually located closer to the franchisee than the franchisor.

Suppliers: The individuals or companies from which franchisees purchase products or services to operate the franchise. The franchisor generally requires the franchisee to purchase supplies from an approved list of suppliers. Sometimes the franchisor itself is the sole supplier.

Training: The initial and ongoing instruction provided by the franchisor to franchisees to teach them the business and operating systems. Training is also given to trouble-shoot problems and introduce new products or procedures to the franchise system.

Transfer Fee: When a franchisee sells a franchise to a new owner, he or she pays this fee to the franchisor.

UFOC (Uniform Franchise Offering Circular): The disclosure document, required by the FTC, that all franchisors must present to all serious potential franchisees, at least 10 business days before a franchise is acquired.

Working Capital: The money needed to operate a new franchise until the business breaks even or shows a profit.

Sample Franchise Agreement
(Excerpt)

LABRADOR FRANCHISES, INC.

FRANCHISE AGREEMENT

TABLE OF CONTENTS

I. DEFINITIONS

II. GRANT

III. FRANCHISED LOCATION; NO TERRITORIAL RIGHTS

IV. TERM AND RENEWAL

V. FRANCHISE LOCATION DEVELOPMENT AND OPENING DATE

VI. TRAINING

VII. PROPRIETARY MARKS

VIII. MANUAL

IX. CONFIDENTIAL INFORMATION DEFINED

X. ADVERTISING

XI. PAYMENTS

XII. ACCOUNTING AND RECORDS

XIII. STANDARDS OF QUALITY AND PERFORMANCE

XIV. COMPANY'S OPERATIONS ASSISTANCE

XV. INSURANCE

XVI. COVENANTS

XVII. DEFAULT AND TERMINATION

XVIII. RIGHTS AND DUTIES OF PARTIES UPON EXPIRATION

XIX. ASSIGNMENT AND TRANSFER

XX. RELATIONSHIP OF PARTIES; INDEMNIFICATION

XXI. GUARANTEE

XXII. JUDICIAL RELIEF

XXIII. ACKNOWLEDGEMENTS

XXIV. MISCELLANEOUS

ATTACHMENTS

Attachment A: The Franchised Location

Attachment B: Authorization Agreement for Pre-Arranged Payments (Direct Debit)

Attachment C: Guarantee

Attachment D: State Specific Amendments

FRANCHISE AGREEMENT

This Franchise Agreement (the "**Agreement**") is made and entered into on _____ _____, ____ (the "**Effective Date**") by and between LABRADOR FRANCHISES, INC., a California corporation ("**FRANCHISOR**") and _____

_____
("**FRANCHISEE**") with reference to the following facts:

      A.   FRANCHISOR owns the PET DEPOT® trade name and service mark, as well as in other trademarks, service marks, logos and commercial symbols which identify and are used in connection with the development, operation and marketing of PET DEPOT® stores (the "**Proprietary Marks**").

      B.   FRANCHISOR owns and has the perpetual license to use and sublicense certain business methods for the development and operation of retail pet stores featuring pet food, pet supplies, pets for sale, veterinary services, grooming services and other related services to the general public. These business methods include, without limitation, distinctive signs and store design specifications; interior and exterior imaging requirements; uniform operating, merchandising and marketing methods; mandatory products and supplies, including products which are specially formulated or branded for FRANCHISOR, which FRANCHISOR refers to as the "**Proprietary Products**" and confidential information and trade secrets. These business methods encompass all aspects of developing, operating and marketing PET DEPOT® stores and are referred to in this Agreement as the "**System**."

      C.   FRANCHISOR reserves the right to modify the System and the Proprietary Marks in its sole discretion as often, and at such times, as it believes will best promote PET DEPOT® to the public.

      D.   FRANCHISEE desires to obtain a franchise and license to use the System and the Proprietary Marks in the operation of a PET DEPOT® store, and FRANCHISOR is willing to grant a license to FRANCHISEE on the terms and conditions of this Agreement.

      NOW, THEREFORE, THE PARTIES AGREE AS FOLLOWS:
I.   **DEFINITIONS**

      In addition to definitions incorporated in the body of this Agreement, the following capitalized terms in this Agreement are defined as follows:

      A.   "**Accounting Period**" means the specific period that FRANCHISOR designates from time to time in the Manual or otherwise in writing for purposes of FRANCHISEE's financial reporting or payment obligations described in this Agreement. For example, an Accounting Period may, in FRANCHISOR's discretion, be based on a calendar month, a quarterly financial calendar (which may, or may not be subdivided into blocks of weeks, e.g., 4 weeks, 4 weeks and 5 weeks), or a shorter or longer time period that FRAN-CHISOR selects in its discretion. FRANCHISOR may designate different Accounting Periods for purposes of paying fees and for discharging reporting obligations under this Agreement.

B.   **"Affiliate"** or **"Affiliates"** mean an entity or entities that control, are controlled by, or are under common control with, a party to this Agreement.

C.   **"Applicable Law"** means and includes applicable common law and all statutes, laws, rules, regulations, ordinances, policies and procedures established by any governmental authority with jurisdiction over the operation of the Franchised Unit that are in effect on or after the Effective Date, as they may be amended from time to time. Applicable Laws includes, without limitation, those relating to building permits and zoning requirements applicable to the use, occupancy and development of the Franchised Location; business licensing requirements; hazardous waste; occupational hazards and health; consumer protection; trade regulation; worker's compensation; unemployment insurance; withholding and payment of Federal and State income taxes and social security taxes; collection and reporting of sales taxes; and the Americans with Disabilities Act.

D.   **"Calendar Year"** means the twelve (12) month period starting on January 1 and ending on December 31.

E.   **"Controlling Interest"** means the possession, directly or indirectly, of power to direct, or cause a change in the direction of, the management and policies of a business entity. FRANCHISOR shall consider whether a transfer, either alone or together with all other previous, simultaneous or proposed transfers, would have the effect of transferring, in the aggregate, a sufficient number of the equity or voting interests of business entity to enable the purchaser or transferee to direct, or cause a change in the direction of, the management and policies of the business entity. For purposes of this Agreement, any person who qualifies as a Primary Owner shall be deemed to own a Controlling Interest.

F.   **"Effective Date"** is the date indicated on Page 1 of this Agreement.

G.   **"Franchised Unit"** means the one PET DEPOT® store that is the subject of this Agreement.

H.   **"Franchised Location"** means the business premises approved by FRANCHISOR for the operation of the PET DEPOT® store that is the subject of this Agreement, having the address shown on **Attachment A**.

I.   **"Lease"** refers to the written agreement by and between FRANCHISEE (i) the owner of the real property business premises where the Franchised Location is situated; or (ii) FRANCHISOR's Affiliate, as sublessor, which grants FRANCHISEE the right to occupy and use the Franchised Location for the operation of a PET DEPOT® store.

J.   **"Lease Assignment Agreement"** means the written agreement by and between FRANCHISEE and the landlord of the Franchised Location that adds specific terms and conditions required by FRANCHISOR to the Lease and grants FRANCHISOR the right, but not the obligation, to accept an assignment of the Lease under stated conditions.

K.   **"Malls"** include regional shopping malls, discount outlet malls and pedestrian shopping destinations, whether or not the Mall is open on the Effective Date or first opens for business after the Effective Date. Regional shopping malls refer to an integrated multiple tenant building or buildings designated by a common name providing a physical destination for retail transactions, with one or more anchor tenants and dedicated parking facilities.

L.   **"Manual"** refers to all of the confidential operating manuals and other written materials loaned to FRANCHISEE in confidence during the Term.

M.   **"Non-Proprietary Products"** refers to all pet food, pet supplies, fixtures, furnishings, equipment, packaging, and merchandise, other than Proprietary Products, authorized by FRANCHISOR which FRANCHISEE may, or must, use, offer, sell or promote in operating the Franchised Unit.

N.   **"Primary Owner"** refers to any person who owns at least twenty-five percent (25%) of the outstanding equity or voting interests of a FRANCHISEE that is a business entity.

O.   **"Proprietary Products"** refers to (i) all products and merchandise (a) manufactured by, or for, FRANCHISOR or FRANCHISOR's Affiliates in accordance with proprietary recipes, specifications or formulas, or (b) displaying any of the Proprietary Marks and promoted as a PET DEPOT® brand item; and (ii) uniforms displaying any of the Proprietary Marks.

P.   **"World Wide Web"** means that portion of the Internet used primarily as a commercial computer network by the general public, and any successor technology, whether now existing or developed after the Effective Date, that enables the general public to purchase goods or services from merchant-controlled World Wide Web sites or through other electronic means.

II.   GRANT

A.   <u>**Award of Rights**</u>. FRANCHISOR hereby awards to FRANCHISEE, and FRANCHISEE accepts, the right and license to use the System and the Proprietary Marks in connection with the operation of the Franchised Unit at the Franchised Location, on the terms and conditions of this Agreement.

1.   FRANCHISEE shall not relocate the Franchised Unit except in accordance with this Agreement.

2.   In accepting the award of rights, FRANCHISEE agrees at all times to faithfully, honestly and diligently perform its obligations under this Agreement and to continuously exert its best efforts to promote and enhance the Franchised Unit and the goodwill associated with the Proprietary Marks and the System.

B.   **Limitations**.

1.   FRANCHISOR grants FRANCHISEE no rights other than the rights expressly stated in this Agreement. FRANCHISEE's use of the System or the Proprietary Marks for any purpose, or in any manner, not permitted by this Agreement shall constitute a breach of this Agreement.

2.   The franchise and license awarded to FRANCHISEE apply to the Franchised Location, and to no other location.

3.   Nothing in this Agreement gives FRANCHISEE the right to sublicense the use of the Proprietary Marks or the System to others.

4.   Nothing in this Agreement gives FRANCHISEE the right to object to FRANCHISOR's award of franchises or development rights to others.

5.   Nothing in this Agreement gives FRANCHISEE an interest in FRANCHISOR or the right to participate in FRANCHISOR's business activities, investment or corporate opportunities.

6.   This Agreement authorizes FRANCHISEE to engage only in retail transactions of authorized products and services to customers for their own use and consumption at the Franchised Location; provided, however, FRANCHISEE may accept telephone orders for sales delivered from the Franchised Location to the customer's designated address.

7.   FRANCHISEE shall not engage in wholesale sales or distribution of products or services of any kind. The term "**wholesale sales or distribution**" means the direct or indirect sale of products or services to a third party for resale or further distribution through any trade method or trade channel. FRANCHISEE shall not maintain a World Wide Web site or otherwise maintain a presence or advertise using any public computer network in connection with the Franchised Unit. FRANCHISEE shall not advertise or sell merchandise or services by mail order, catalog sales or comparable methods that solicit business from customers by means not requiring the customer's physical presence in the Franchised Location to complete the transaction; except for telephone orders delivered from the Franchised Location to the customer's designated address.

C.   **Improvements; Duty to Conform to Modifications**.

1.   Any improvements, modifications or additions which FRANCHISOR makes to the System, or which become associated with the System, including, without limitation, ideas suggested or initiated by FRANCHISEE, shall inure to the benefit, and become the exclusive property, of FRANCHISOR. FRANCHISEE hereby assigns to FRANCHISOR or its designee all intellectual property rights, including, without limitation, all copyrights, in and to any improvements or works which FRANCHISEE may create, acquire or obtain in operating the Franchised Unit. FRANCHISEE understands and agrees that nothing in this Agreement shall constitute or be construed as FRANCHISOR's consent or permission to FRANCHISEE modifying the System. Any modification which FRANCHISEE desires to propose or make to the System shall require FRANCHISOR's prior written consent.

2.   Any goodwill resulting from FRANCHISEE's use of the Proprietary Marks or the System shall inure to the exclusive benefit of FRANCHISOR. This Agreement confers no goodwill or other interest in the Proprietary Marks or the System upon FRANCHISEE, except a license to use the Proprietary Marks and the System during the Term subject to the terms and conditions stated in this Agreement.

3.   FRANCHISEE understands and agrees that FRANCHISOR may modify the System from time to time in its sole discretion as often as FRANCHISOR believes, in the exercise of reasonable business judgment, is necessary to best promote PET DEPOT®, as a chain, to the public. In the event of any change to the System, FRANCHISOR shall give FRANCHISEE written notice of the change. FRANCHISEE shall, at its own cost and expense, promptly adopt and use only those parts of the System specified by FRANCHISOR and shall promptly discontinue the use of those parts of the System which FRANCHISOR directs are to be discontinued. FRANCHISEE shall not change, modify or alter the System in any way, except as FRANCHISOR directs.

D.   **Deviations from the System**.

A.   FRANCHISOR, in its sole discretion, may allow other franchisees and licensees to deviate from the System in individual cases. FRANCHISEE understands and agrees that it has no right to object to any variances that FRANCHISOR may allow to itself, FRANCHISOR's Affiliates or other franchisees, and has no claim against FRANCHISOR for not enforcing the standards of the System uniformly. FRANCHISEE understands and agrees that FRANCHISOR has no obligation to waive, make any exceptions to, or permit FRANCHISEE to deviate from, the uniform standards of the System. Any exception or deviation that FRANCHISOR does allow FRANCHISEE must be stated in writing and executed by FRANCHISOR in order to be enforceable against FRANCHISOR.

B. **Additional Franchises**. FRANCHISEE understands and agrees that this Agreement does not grant FRANCHISEE any implied or preferential right of any kind to acquire an additional franchise to operate another Franchised Unit.

III. FRANCHISED LOCATION; NO TERRITORIAL RIGHTS

A. **Selection of Franchised Location**.

1. FRANCHISEE shall select the Franchised Location, subject to FRANCHISOR's approval, pursuant to the procedures stated in this Article III.

a. In evaluating potential sites, FRANCHISEE shall consider FRANCHISOR's current site selection criteria set forth in the Manual as well as FRANCHISOR's current prototype floor plans and specifications for the design, appearance and leasehold improvements of a typical PET DEPOT®, which FRANCHISOR shall provide to FRANCHISEE, without charge, following the parties' execution of this Agreement.

b. To obtain FRANCHISOR's approval of a proposed site, FRANCHISEE shall submit a written site proposal to FRANCHISOR, in the form indicated in the Manual. FRANCHISEE's site proposal shall be accompanied by a letter of intent or other evidence satisfactory to FRANCHISOR which confirms the owner of the Franchised Location's willingness to offer FRANCHISEE a lease and to execute an Addendum to Lease in the form required by FRANCHISOR.

c. Following receipt of FRANCHISEE's written site proposal FRANCHISOR may, in its discretion, make an on-site visit to the proposed site at its expense if FRANCHISOR reasonably believes that physical inspection of the demographic conditions of the area, or the proposed site, is necessary or desirable to evaluate FRANCHISEE's proposal. FRANCHISEE understands and agrees that the on-site visit is at FRANCHISOR's option and not required by this Agreement.

d. FRANCHISOR shall have twenty-one (21) days following receipt of FRANCHISEE's completed site proposal to complete any site visit that it chooses to make and approve or disapprove the proposed site by giving written notice to FRANCHISEE. If FRANCHISEE proposes more than one site, FRANCHISOR need only approve one site, or it may disapprove all proposed sites. FRANCHISEE understands and agrees that FRANCHISOR's failure to give timely notice of approval shall constitute FRANCHISOR's disapproval of all sites proposed by FRANCHISEE. FRANCHISOR failure to give timely notice of approval shall constitute FRANCHISOR's disapproval of the site.

e.   FRANCHISEE understands and agrees that:

(1)   It is solely responsible for site selection and for negotiation of a lease for the Franchised Location;

(2)   Neither FRANCHISOR's proposal or approval of a site constitute a guarantee or warranty that operation of a PET DEPOT® store located at the approved site will be successful or profitable. FRANCHISOR's approval of a site signifies only that the site meets FRANCHISOR's current site criteria; and

(3)   Neither FRANCHISOR's proposal or approval of a site certify that FRANCHISEE's development, use or occupancy of the proposed site as a PET DEPOT® store will conform to applicable local laws, codes or permit requirements. FRANCHISEE understands and agrees that it is solely responsible for investigating and complying with all applicable local laws, codes and permit requirements concerning its development and occupancy of each Franchised Location.

f.   When FRANCHISOR notifies FRANCHISEE of its approval of FRANCHISEE's proposed site, Franchisor will notify FRANCHISEE of the approval via written letter.

g.   Promptly following FRANCHISOR's approval of the Franchised Location, FRANCHISEE shall (i) execute a Lease and a Lease Assignment Agreement with the real property owner or master landlord of the Franchised Location and FRANCHISOR, and (ii) deliver to FRANCHISOR a copy of the fully-executed Lease and Lease Assignment Agreement. If FRANCHISOR determines, in its discretion, to review the Lease and incurs legal fees in connection with such review, FRANCHISEE shall pay FRANCHISOR's legal fees to do so; however the costs for same will not exceed $1,200.

h.   FRANCHISOR may terminate this Agreement if FRANCHISEE fails to secure FRANCHISOR's approval of the Franchised Location and deliver the executed Lease and Lease Assignment Agreement to FRANCHISOR within twenty-four (24) months after the Effective Date. If this Agreement terminates for the reasons stated in this Paragraph III(A)(1(h), FRANCHISEE shall not be entitled to a refund of any fees or other payments paid to FRANCHISOR or FRANCHISOR's Affiliates.

B.   **No Territorial Rights**.

1.   FRANCHISEE understands and agrees that nothing in this Agreement grants to FRANCHISEE any area, market or territorial rights or protection of any kind. FRANCHISOR may open or operate, or grant others, including (without limitation) FRANCHISOR's Affiliates, the right to open or operate, PET DEPOT® anywhere regardless of the proximity to the Franchised Location.

2.   FRANCHISEE understands and agrees that (i) the rights and license awarded to FRANCHISEE are non-exclusive; (ii) FRANCHISOR reserves all other rights to use the Proprietary Marks and the System for all purposes; (iii) FRANCHISEE shall have no right to enjoin or be compensated for the opening or operation of another PET DEPOT® or for any other type of use of the System regardless of its proximity to the Franchised Location; and (iv):

a.   FRANCHISOR expressly reserves the absolute right to distribute any and all Non-Proprietary Products and Proprietary Products using the Proprietary Marks through all channels of trade and distribution, regardless of whether (i) the channel of distribution now exists or is developed after the Effective Date, or (ii) the Non-Proprietary Products or Proprietary Products are now, or in the future, authorized for sale at PET DEPOT® stores.

b.   As examples of FRANCHISOR's reserved rights, and not by limitation, FRANCHISOR may directly or indirectly, itself or through FRANCHISOR's Affiliates, licensees, franchisees, assignees, agents and others:

(1)   Produce, license, distribute, market and sell products and services of any kind, including, without limitation, Proprietary Products, through other retail and wholesale channels of distribution, including, without limitation, by means of electronic communication, the World Wide Web, mail order catalogues, direct mail advertising, and comparable methods that solicit business from customers by means not requiring a physical transaction at a retail or wholesale location;

(2)   Produce, license, distribute, market and sell products and services of any kind, including, without limitation, Proprietary Products, from supermarkets, health food stores and other wholesale and retail food stores owned by third parties that are not licensed to do business under the Proprietary Marks;

(3)   Operate other kinds of businesses under the Proprietary Marks that do not feature pet services, pet food, veterinary services, pet grooming services, Proprietary Products, or other products and services similar to those now, or in the future, featured at PET DEPOT® stores;

(4)   Operate other retail and wholesale concepts under trade names dissimilar to the Proprietary Marks that compete with PET DEPOT® stores, including retail and wholesale businesses that feature pet services, pet food, veterinary services, pet grooming services, or other products and services similar to those now, or in the future, featured at PET DEPOT® stores; and

(5)   To own, acquire, establish and/or operate and grant others the right to develop, own, operate and issue franchises and licenses to others to develop, own and operate other methods and channels of distribution utilizing the

Proprietary Marks and the System, including, without limitation, toll-free "1-800", "1-888" and "1-877" telephone numbers, domain names, URLs, on-line computer networks and services, the Internet, kiosks, carts, concessions, satellite units, other mobile, remote, limited service or non-permanent facilities or other retail operations as a part of larger retail venues such as department stores, supermarkets, shopping malls or in public areas such as amusement parks, airports, train stations, public facilities, college and school campuses, arenas, stadiums, hospitals, office buildings, convention centers and military bases.

      C.   **Relocation**.

         1.   If (i) the Lease expires or terminates for reasons other than FRANCHISEE's breach; (ii) the Franchised Location or building in which the Franchised Unit is located is destroyed, condemned or otherwise rendered unusable; or (iii) the parties mutually believe that relocation will increase the business potential of the franchise, FRANCHISEE agrees to relocate the Franchised Unit, at Franchisee's sole expense, to a new location selected by FRANCHISEE, and approved by FRANCHISOR, in accordance with FRANCHISOR's then-current site selection procedures as specified in the Manual. The parties shall amend **Attachment A** to reflect the address of the new Franchised Location.

         2.   At FRANCHISEE's sole expense, FRANCHISEE shall construct and develop the new premises to conform to FRANCHISOR's then-current specifications for design, appearance and leasehold improvements for new PET DEPOT® stores, and remove any signs or other property from the original Franchised Location which identified the original Franchised Location as part of the System.

         3.   FRANCHISEE shall complete relocation without any interruption in the continuous operation of the Franchised Unit unless FRANCHISOR's prior written consent is obtained. In the event FRANCHISOR consents to a disruption in operations and such operations cease, then FRANCHISEE agrees that, until operations resume at the new location: (i) the term of this Agreement shall not be abated, and (ii) FRANCHISEE shall remain liable to pay Royalty Fees and Advertising Fees in an amount equal to the average amount paid by FRANCHISEE during the four (4) calendar quarters immediately preceding the date that operations cease or the shorter period that FRANCHISEE has been in business at the original Franchised Location.

IV.   **TERM AND RENEWAL**

      A.   **Term**. This Agreement shall begin on the Effective Date and shall expire without notice ten (10) years from the Effective Date, unless this Agreement is sooner terminated as provided herein (the ten (10) year period is referred to as the "**Term**").

      B.   **Renewal Term**. Provided FRANCHISOR is granting new franchises at the time when FRANCHISEE is permitted to exercise each renewal option granted by this Agreement, FRANCHISEE may, at its option, renew the franchise for two (2) successive options each for an additional ten (10) years (each option is for a period described as the "**Renewal Term**" or individually, and successively, as the "**First Renewal Term**" and "**Second Renewal Term**"). To exercise each renewal option, FRANCHISEE must comply with the following conditions:

1. FRANCHISEE must give FRANCHISOR written notice of FRANCHISEE's election to renew (the "**Renewal Notice**") at least nine (9) months, but not more than twelve (12) months, before the end of the Term or the applicable Renewal Term. Each successive Renewal Term shall begin on the day immediately following the expiration of the Term or prior Renewal Term. FRANCHISEE shall have no right to exercise the Second Renewal Term unless FRANCHISEE has exercised the First Renewal Term.

2. FRANCHISEE's Renewal Notice must each be accompanied by a non-refundable renewal fee equal to twenty-five percent (25%) of the Initial Franchise Fee that FRANCHISOR is then charging for new PET DEPOT® franchises in the United States.

3. FRANCHISEE must not be in default under this Agreement or any successor Franchise Agreement or any other agreement with FRANCHISOR or FRANCHISOR's Affiliates at the time it gives its Renewal Notice or on the first day of the applicable Renewal Term. Further, FRANCHISEE must not have received more than three (3) notices of default during any twenty-four (24) month period during the Term or then-current Renewal Term.

4. To exercise each renewal option, FRANCHISEE shall execute FRANCHISOR's then-current form of Franchise Agreement for a ten (10) year term, which agreement shall supersede this Agreement in all respects; provided, however, FRANCHISEE shall have no additional renewal rights even if the renewal Franchise Agreement provides for a renewal option that is different than this Agreement. FRANCHISEE shall not be required to pay the Initial Franchise Fee stated in each renewal Franchise Agreement, but instead shall pay the renewal fee stated in this Agreement. Exercise of the first renewal option shall result in an extension of this Agreement for an additional ten (10) years only. FRANCHISEE understands that the renewal Franchise Agreement it is required to execute may be materially different than this Agreement, including, without limitation, requiring payment of additional or different fees to FRANCHISOR.

5. FRANCHISEE shall satisfy FRANCHISOR's then-current training requirements for renewing franchisees.

6. FRANCHISEE shall satisfy FRANCHISOR's then-current appearance and design standards and equipment specifications that apply to new

PET DEPOT® stores, including (without limitation) conforming the Franchised Unit to FRANCHISOR's then-current requirements relating to decoration, furnishings, merchandise, services and inventory and accounting systems.

    7. FRANCHISEE shall execute a General Release, in a form prescribed by FRANCHISOR, of any and all claims which FRANCHISEE may have or believes to have against FRANCHISOR and its Affiliates and their respective officers, directors, agents and employees, whether the claims are known or unknown, which are based on, arise from or relate to this Agreement, the Franchised Unit or the Franchised Location, as well as claims, known or unknown, which are not based on, do not arise from or do not relate to this Agreement, the Franchised Unit or the Franchised Location but which relate to other franchise agreements, stores, franchised locations and other agreements between FRANCHISOR and its Affiliates and FRANCHISEE which arose on or before the date of the General Release, including, without limitation, all obligations, liabilities, demands, costs, expenses, damages, claims, actions and causes of action, of whatever nature, character or description, arising under federal, state and local laws, rules and ordinances.

  C. **Ineffective Exercise of Renewal Option**. FRANCHISEE's failure to deliver the agreements and release required by this Paragraph within thirty (30) days after FRANCHISOR delivers them to FRANCHISEE shall be deemed an election by FRANCHISEE not to exercise the applicable renewal option.

  D. **Extension**. If FRANCHISOR is in the process of revising, amending or renewing its franchise disclosure documents or registration to sell franchises in the state where the Franchised Unit is located, or, under Applicable Law, cannot lawfully offer FRANCHISEE its then-current form of Franchise Agreement at the time FRANCHISEE delivers a Renewal Notice, FRANCHISOR may, in its sole and absolute discretion, offer to extend the terms and conditions of this Agreement on a day-to-day basis following the expiration of a Renewal Term for as long as FRANCHISOR deems necessary so that FRANCHISOR may lawfully offer its then-current form of Franchise Agreement; provided, however, nothing in this Paragraph IV(D) shall require FRANCHISOR to extend this Agreement if, at the time FRANCHISEE delivers a Renewal Notice (i) FRANCHISOR is not granting new franchises, or (ii) FRANCHISEE is in default under this Agreement or a successor Franchise Agreement or under any other agreement with FRANCHISOR or FRANCHISOR's Affiliates.

  E. **Failure to Satisfy Renewal Conditions**. If any of the renewal conditions are not timely satisfied, this Agreement will expire on the last day of the Term without further notice from FRANCHISOR; provided, however, FRANCHISEE shall remain obligated to comply with all provisions of this Agreement which expressly, or by their nature, survive the expiration or termination of this Agreement.

V. FRANCHISE LOCATION DEVELOPMENT AND OPENING DATE

A. Franchisee's Design Plans.

1. FRANCHISOR shall provide FRANCHISEE with a set of FRANCHISOR's prototype plans and specifications for a typical PET DEPOT® after the parties execute this Agreement, which FRANCHISEE shall use to evaluate potential sites and select the Franchised Location.

2. At FRANCHISEE's sole expense, FRANCHISEE shall pay for the services of a FRANCHISOR approved, licensed and qualified architect or other construction personnel to prepare design and construction plans ("**Franchisee's Design Plans**") that adapt FRANCHISOR's prototype plans and specifications to the specific dimensions and conditions of the Franchised Location and to the requirements of the Lease and Applicable Laws. At a minimum, the Franchisee's Design Plans shall address, without limitation, exterior design and lighting plans, interior design and layout plans, and specifications for the items of equipment, fixtures, furniture, signs, supplies, utilities, materials and decorations that FRANCHISEE intends to install and use in the Franchised Location, together with such other information as may be specified in the Manual.

3. FRANCHISEE shall submit Franchisee's Design Plans to FRANCHISOR for approval by FRANCHISOR or FRANCHISOR's architect. FRANCHISOR shall promptly review the Franchisee's Design Plans and may reject or accept the Franchisee's Design Plans completely, or approve FRANCHISEE's Permitted Plans subject to specified modifications. FRANCHISOR shall communicate its decision in writing within fifteen (15) days after receipt of plans.

B. Development of Franchised Location.

1. FRANCHISEE shall cause all construction and other development work to be carried out in compliance with the version of the Franchisee's Design Plans that FRANCHISOR approves, including any required specified modifications. FRANCHISEE is solely responsible for procuring all equipment, fixtures, furniture, computer systems, signs, supplies, materials and supplies required for the development and operation of the Franchised Unit from designated or approved suppliers. FRANCHISEE shall not make any material changes to the approved Franchisee's Design Plans without first submitting the changes to FRANCHISOR for its approval. FRANCHISEE shall furthermore cause all construction and development work to conform with the Lease and Applicable Laws, including, without limitation, all government and utility permit requirements (such as, for example, zoning, sanitation, building, utility and sign permits). FRANCHISEE shall complete development of the Franchised Location diligently, expeditiously and in a first-class manner. FRANCHISOR shall have access to the Franchised Location to inspect the work and performance by FRANCHISEE's construction personnel.

2.   FRANCHISEE understands and agrees that it is solely responsible for selecting competent construction personnel and for supervising, and for the acts and omissions of, its construction personnel. FRANCHISEE shall obtain all customary contractors lien waivers for the work performed.

3.   FRANCHISOR shall have no responsibility for any delays in development or opening of the Franchised Unit or for any loss resulting from the design of the Franchised Location. FRANCHISEE understands and agrees that if FRANCHISOR inspects the work and performance of FRANCHISEE's construction personnel, the inspection is not for purposes of reviewing or certifying that development is in compliance with the Lease or Applicable Laws, but solely to evaluate that development conforms with the set of FRANCHISEE's Design Plans that FRANCHISOR has approved and otherwise with FRANCHISOR's specifications for design, appearance and leasehold improvements.

4.   FRANCHISEE may not open the Franchised Location for business to the public under the Proprietary Marks unless and until FRANCHISOR issues a written completion certificate. The certificate shall signify that FRANCHISOR finds that the Franchised Location, as built, substantially conforms to FRANCHISOR's design specifications.

C.   **Opening Date**.

1.   FRANCHISOR may terminate this Agreement effective upon written notice to FRANCHISEE if FRANCHISEE fails to complete construction of improvements and open for business to the public by no later than twelve (12) months after the Effective Date (the "**Opening Date**"). If this Agreement terminates for the reasons stated in this Paragraph V(C)(1), FRANCHISEE shall not be entitled to a refund of any fees or other payments paid to FRANCHISOR or FRANCHISOR's Affiliates.

2.   FRANCHISOR may extend the Opening Date if FRANCHISOR determines that the Franchised Location's opening has been, or will be, delayed due to strikes, material shortages, fires, floods, earthquakes or other acts of God or by force of law ("**Force Majeure**"), which FRANCHISEE could not have reasonably avoided. The Opening Date shall be extended by an amount of time equal to the time period during which the Force Majeure shall have existed. The determination that an event of Force Majeure has occurred shall be made solely by FRANCHISOR based upon the event causing the delay. FRANCHISOR shall identify the extended Opening Date in writing delivered to FRANCHISEE. If FRANCHISOR extends the Opening Date, FRANCHISEE must open for business to the public, by no later than the extended Opening Date.

D.   **Relocation**.

    1.   If (i) the Lease expires or terminates for reasons other than FRANCHISEE's breach; (ii) the Franchised Location or building in which the Franchised Unit is located is destroyed, condemned or otherwise rendered unusable; or (iii) the parties' mutually believe that relocation will increase the business potential of the franchise, FRANCHISEE agrees to relocate the Franchised Unit, at FRANCHISEE's sole expense, to a new location selected by FRANCHISEE, and approved by FRANCHISOR, in accordance with FRANCHISOR's then-current site selection procedures as specified in the Manual. At FRANCHISEE's sole expense, FRANCHISEE shall construct and develop the new premises to conform to FRANCHISOR's then-current specifications for design, appearance and leasehold improvements for new PET DEPOT® stores, and remove any signs or other property from the original Franchised Location which identified the original Franchised Location as part of the System.

    2.   FRANCHISEE shall complete relocation without any interruption in the continuous operation of the Franchised Unit unless FRANCHISOR's prior written consent is obtained. In the event FRANCHISOR consents to a disruption in operations and such operations cease, then FRANCHISEE agrees that, until operations resume at the new location: (i) the term of this Agreement shall not be abated, and (ii) FRANCHISEE shall remain liable to pay Royalty Fees and Advertising Fees in an amount equal to the average amount paid by FRANCHISEE during the two (2) calendar quarters immediately preceding the date that operations cease or the shorter period that FRANCHISEE has been in business at the original Franchised Location.

VI.   TRAINING

A.   **Initial Training Program**.

    1.   As of the Effective Date, FRANCHISOR's initial training program consists of two parts: (i) approximately eighty (80) hours of administrative and operational training ("**Phase I Training**") conducted in a classroom environment and/or at an operating PET DEPOT® that FRANCHISOR shall designate; and (ii) approximately forty (40) hours of on-site instruction at the Franchised Location at a mutually scheduled time for one week before, or the period including, the Opening Date ("**Phase II Training**"). FRANCHISOR reserves the right to modify FRANCHISOR's initial training program at any time without notice, and to determine the content, duration and manner of conducting the initial training program in FRANCHISOR's sole discretion.

    2.   FRANCHISOR shall provide the initial training program at no extra charge only once, before the opening of the Franchised Unit, to two (2) persons, provided both attend the same initial training sessions. FRANCHISEE may enroll additional trainees in the initial training program under the conditions specified in this Agreement, so

long as such additional trainees attend the same initial training sessions and FRANCHI-SEE pays FRANCHISOR the sum of $500 for each additional trainee. FRANCHISOR shall not be obligated to provide an initial training program in connection with FRAN-CHISEE's exercise of any renewal option.

3.   At a minimum, either FRANCHISEE, FRANCHISEE's Primary Owner, or a senior operations employee acceptable to FRANCHISOR who will have general management and supervisory responsibilities for one or more PET DEPOT® stores, must successfully complete both Phase I and Phase II Training before the opening of the Franchised Unit and qualify as a Certified Manager, signifying that the person is qualified to train FRANCHISEE's other store-level managers and employees. If, at the end of the initial training program, this person fails to demonstrate the requisite competency to operate and manage a PET DEPOT® store in FRANCHISOR's judgment, based on FRANCHI-SOR's sole subjective evaluation, FRANCHISOR may terminate this Agreement. Termination shall be effective upon delivery of written notice.

4.   At all times during the Term, FRANCHISEE must employ at least one Certified Manager. Notwithstanding FRANCHISOR's designation, FRANCHI-SOR shall have no responsibility for the operating results of the Franchised Unit or the performance of FRANCHISEE's employees. FRANCHISOR may change the criteria for designation as a Certified Manager at any time effective upon notice to FRANCHI-SEE. FRANCHISOR's notice shall specify the additional training and other requirements applicable to new Certified Managers which existing Certified Managers must complete to maintain their designation as a Certified Manager. FRANCHISOR shall allow existing Certified Managers ninety (90) days after the new criteria become effective in which to satisfy the additional training and other requirements without suffering a lapse in their designation as a Certified Manager.

B.   **Additional Training**.

1.   All newly hired and replacement management personnel shall demonstrate the requisite competency to operate and manage a PET DEPOT® store in FRANCHISOR's judgment, based on FRANCHISOR's sole subjective evaluation.

2.   FRANCHISEE may request permission (i) to send additional persons to the initial training program, (ii) to enroll its employees in other initial training program sessions during the Term or in connection with the opening of subsequent PET DEPOT® stores, (iii) to extend the initial training program for a longer period, or (iv) to receive additional training and on-site assistance after the Opening Date. FRANCHISEE understands and agrees that all additional training shall be at mutually scheduled times, subject to space availability and FRANCHISOR's other training commitments, and that, as a condition to receiving additional training, FRANCHISEE must pay FRANCHISOR's then-current per person training fees stated in the Manual. In connection with additional

on-site instruction, FRANCHISEE shall also reimburse FRANCHISOR for its reasonable travel-related expenses, including, without limitation, expenses for air and ground transportation, lodging, meals, and personal charges.

3.   FRANCHISOR reserves the right to require that FRANCHISEE's Certified Managers or other designated personnel attend specified additional training programs; provided, however, FRANCHISOR shall not require that more than two (2) persons designated by FRANCHISOR complete more than one additional training program of up to three (3) days during any twelve (12) month period. As a condition to completing mandatory additional training, FRANCHISEE shall pay FRANCHISOR's then current per person training fees.

4.   In connection with any event of transfer, FRANCHISEE or the proposed transferee shall be solely responsible for all personal expenses that the proposed transferee and its employees incur in connection with such training. FRANCHISEE shall remain responsible for operation and management of the Franchised Unit until the proposed transferee and its personnel complete and demonstrate the requisite competency to operate and manage a PET DEPOT® store in FRANCHISOR's judgment, based on FRANCHISOR's sole subjective evaluation.

C.   **Additional Provisions**.

1.   FRANCHISOR shall schedule all training, including, without limitation, on-site Training, according to its training schedule, subject to space availability.

2.   FRANCHISEE understands and agrees that (i) it is solely responsible for all personal expenses that it and its employees incur to attend any and all training provided by FRANCHISOR whether before or after the Opening Date, including, without limitation, costs for air and ground transportation, lodging, meals, personal expenses and salaries, and (ii) that FRANCHISOR shall pay no compensation for any services performed by trainees in connection with any training program provided by FRANCHISOR.

—End of Sample Franchise Agreement Excerpt—

Index

A

Accountant, 49, 50, 87
Advertising, 4, 28, 32, 55-57, 59, 85, 87, 88, 96, 162
American Association of Franchisees and Dealers (AAFD)
    (*www.aafd.org*), 7, 44, 53, 66, 103, 125
American Institute of Certified Public Accountants Standards for
    Financial Forecasts or Projections, 91
Area developer, 19-20
Assessment of franchise, 7-8, 51-60, 90-91, 92, 120, 168-69. *See also*
    Investigation (of franchise); Researching (franchises)
Attorney, franchise, 46, 49, 57, 87, 90, 92, 94, 102, 103, 104, 108, 116, 117,
    122, 131
Auditing of franchisee, 22, 88, 113

B

BBB Reliability Reports on franchisors (*www.bbb.org*), 137
Bankruptcies, 97, 141
Brand name (of franchise), 4, 5, 7, 19, 76, 125
Broker, franchise, 21
Business model/system, 2, 5, 7, 76
Business plan, 5, 60, 151, 161-66
Business Plan In A Day (www.planningshop.com), 162
Business Resale Network, 70

C

Capital
    start-up, 74, 81
    working, 50, 84, 85, 88, 147, 151
Cash-flow statements, 70, 166
Chain (vs. franchise), 6
Clothing, 27, 84
Company-owned outlets, 100
    vs. franchises, 53, 58, 59, 90
Competition, 161, 163
Construction/remodeling of franchise location, 83, 87, 88
Consultant, franchise, 22
Costs, associated with franchise, 44, 50, 53
    ongoing, 86-88, 127
    start-up, 7, 10, 11, 47, 74, 77-79, 81, 82-85, 98, 127, 144-47, 151
    UFOC descriptions of, 96
See also Financing; Investment in franchise

D

Disclosure document. *See* Uniform Franchise Offering Circular (UFOC)

"Discovery Day," 133-34

Dispute resolution (between franchisor and franchisee), 100, 123

Due diligence, 5, 103, 121-41
    legitimacy of franchise, 73
    substantiating claims, 72

E

Earnings claim (on UFOC), 90-91, 100, 151

Equipment, 71, 85, 86

F

Federal Trade Commission (FTC), 23, 94, 95, 103

Financial information (about franchises), 70, 90-91, 101

Financial statements, 70, 165-66

Financing, 5, 71, 99, 115, 144-60, 164
    bank loan, 149-52
    credit history, 150
    debt financing, 148
    equity financing, 148
    equity investor, 145
    from franchisor, 145, 152-53
    government, 159
    from partner, 160
    start-up, 144-47, 151

See also Investment in franchise

Finding an Angel Investor In A Day (www.planningshop.com), 157

Fit (between franchisor and franchisee), 21, 42-50, 51, 52, 123, 125, 131-41,
    168

Franchise
    benefits, 2, 4-23
      for franchisees, 5
      for franchisors, 5
    business model, 2
    vs. business opportunity, 64
    vs. chain, 6
    vs. company-owned store, 53, 58, 59, 90
    definition, 6, 11
    drawbacks, 4
    evaluating quality of, 7-8
    existing (acquiring), 70-72
    fastest-growing, 18
    fee, 7, 10, 11, 76, 77-79, 85, 86, 97, 107, 108, 112, 113
    fraudulent, 73
    location, 10, 11, 27, 60, 70, 71, 85, 87, 115, 161, 163
    mobile service, 85
    profitability, 90-91, 123, 126
    rules, 26
    sales from, as percentage of retail sales, 11

sale of, to new owner, 72, 88, 108, 113, 117
sectors, 10, 11, 12-17, 79
vs. small-business, 9
territory, 27, 99, 107, 109, 110, 117
Franchise agreement, 5, 30, 48, 49, 59, 77, 95-96, 101, 102-19, 117, 119, 151, 164
analyzing, 109
finalizing, 119
front-loaded, 108
negotiating, 102, 103-19
non-compete clause, 115
renewal, 118
automatic, 108, 117
fees, 88, 117
vs. UFOC, 102, 103, 105
Franchise fee, 7, 10, 11, 76, 77-79, 85, 86, 97, 107, 108, 112, 113
Franchise Registry (*www.franchiseregistry.com*), 144-45, 150
Franchisee
area developer, 19-20
definition, 4
failures, 57
and family, 37-39, 43, 115
financial security, 28, 38, 45
financial worth required by franchisor, 45
independence (in operating franchise), 26-29, 31, 44
liability, 108-9
lifestyle, 43, 44
master, 20
multi-unit, 19, 20
obligations to franchisor, 98, 108-9, 114
single-unit, 19
stress (of operating franchise), 38-39, 43, 132
sub-franchisee, 21
successful, 9, 30-36, 132, 141
suitability for particular franchise, 43, 44, 52
training of, by franchisor, 4, 5, 22, 54-55, 59, 78, 81, 82-83, 86, 107
Franchisee association, 52-53, 123, 124
Franchisee-franchisor relationship, 21, 27-29, 30, 45, 47, 48, 59, 98, 108-9, 114, 116, 123, 131-41
"Discovery Day," 133-34
dispute resolution, 100, 123
liability of franchisee, 108-9
termination of, 100, 118
trust in, 133, 134
Franchisees, other (current & former), 47, 51, 52, 59, 120
association, 52-53, 123, 124
interviews with, 122-30
listed on UFOC, 95, 100, 124
Franchisor
bankruptcy, 97
business concept, 59
complaints against, 137

Franchisor *(continued)*
    corporate headquarters, 48, 53, 133-34
    definition, 4
    executives, 48, 95, 123, 133
    financial health, 123
    financing provided by, 154
    and franchisee
        control of, 27-29
        expectations of, 140
        financial worth required by franchisor, 45, 140-41
        interviews with, 131
        obligations to, 99, 116
    litigation against, 57, 97, 104, 136
    operating system, 59
    sales representative, 21, 131, 132
    UFOC description of, 97
    undesirable/unethical, 4, 51, 52, 57-58, 95

I

Income (from franchise), 90-91
    fluctuation, 37
    immediate, from existing franchise, 71
    required by franchisee, 45
See also Earnings claim (on UFOC); Profitability (of franchise)
Insurance, 81, 87, 88
International Franchise Association (IFA) *(www.franchise.org)*, 10, 18,
    44, 66, 67, 79, 103
Interviews
    with other franchisees, 122-30
    with franchisor, 131-41
    with similar non-franchised businesses, 126-27
Inventory, 83, 87
Investigation (of franchise), 5, 40, 42-50, 90-91, 92, 120
Investment in franchise, 7, 10, 11, 44, 47, 50, 74, 76, 77-79, 82-85, 98, 127,
    144-60. *See also* Costs, associated with franchise; Financing

L

Lease (for franchise location), 60, 72, 83, 87, 89, 111
Liability (of franchisee), 108-9
Litigation (against franchisor), 57, 97, 104, 136
Loans (to start up franchise), 47, 50, 144-60
    angel investors, 157
    application process, 151-52
    bank, 144-45, 149-52
    friends and family, 155-56
    private investors, 157-58
    SBA-backed, 154
    Small Business Investment Companies (SBICs), 158-59
Location of franchise, 10, 11, 27, 72, 87, 125, 161, 163

M

Maintenance/improvement of franchise location, 86, 111
Marketing, 4, 5, 28, 32, 55-57, 59, 83, 87, 125, 162, 163

N

Negotiating franchise agreement, 103-19

O

Offering circular. *See* Uniform Franchise Offering Circular (UFOC)
Opening, grand (of franchise outlet), 83, 87, 108
Operating standards/system (franchisor's), 28, 59
Owners' association, 52-53, 123, 124, 125

P

Partner, business, 50, 145, 146, 160
Permits, business, 77, 87
Personal guarantee, 108-9, 115
Personnel (of franchise), 43, 71, 88, 162, 164
Product (offered by franchise), 4, 7, 60, 76
    limits imposed by franchisor, 100, 162
Profitability (of franchise), 11, 76, 90-91

R

Registration, of franchise, 101
Renewals (of franchise agreement), 100, 117, 118
Researching (franchises), 5, 40, 42-50, 61-73, 90-91, 92, 120
Revenue. *See* Earnings claim (on UFOC); Income (from franchise)
"Right to cure" provision, 106, 107
Risk, 6, 37-38
Royalties (paid to franchisor), 52, 59, 76, 80-81, 86, 91, 96, 98, 105, 112,
    113, 117

S

Sectors (franchise), 10, 11, 12-17, 79, 84
Service (offered by franchise), 4, 7, 28, 60, 76
    limits imposed by franchisor, 100
Service Corps of Retired Executives (SCORE), 62
Small Business Administration (SBA), 144, 150
Small Business Development Centers (SBDCs), 65
Start-up
    costs, 7, 10, 11, 47, 74, 77-79, 81, 82-85, 98, 127, 144-47, 151
    funding, 144-37
Stress (of operating franchise), 38-39, 43, 132
Success of franchise, 9, 30-36, 132, 141
Supplies, 87
    franchisee purchases from franchisor, 4, 96, 98
    initial, 85
Support (of franchisee by franchisor), 4, 52, 60, 78, 86, 107, 123, 132

T

Taxes, 70, 87

Territory, franchisee's, 27, 99, 107, 109, 110, 117

Trademark, 56, 59, 99

Training of franchisee, 4, 5, 22, 54-55, 59, 78, 81, 82-83, 86, 107

Transfers, 100, 118

    fees, 72, 88, 108

U

Uniform Franchise Offering Circular (UFOC), 8, 11, 23, 46, 47, 48, 49,
    51, 53, 57, 59, 62, 73, 80, 90, 92, 94-101, 131

    vs. franchise agreement, 102, 103, 105

    item-by-item description, 96-101

U.S. Small Business Administration (SBA), 65

W

Websites (for researching franchises), 61-63

    www.aafd.org (American Association of Franchisees and Dealers),
        7, 44, 53, 69

    www.americasbestfranchises.com, 44

    www.areadeveloper.us/mudco/, 67

    www.bbb.org, 69, 137

    www.br-network.com, 70

    www.business.gov, 61

    www.entrepreneur.com, 68

    www.franchise.org (International Franchise Association), 44

    www.franchiseexpo.com, 67

    www.franchisegator.com, 44

    www.franchisehandbook.com, 61

    www.franchisehelp.com, 44

    www.franchise1.com, 61

    www.franchise.org, 68, 69

    www.franchiseshowinfo.com, 66

    www.franchisesolutions.com, 61

    www.franchisetimes.com, 68

    www.franchise-update.com, 67, 68

    www.franmarket.com, 61

    www.inc.com, 69

    www.nase.com, 61

    www.ravingbrands.com, 67

    www.sourcebook-publications.com, 63

    www.wcfexpo.com, 67

    www.worldfranchising.com, 63

Acknowledgments

The Planning Shop would like to thank the staff of the Council of Better Business Bureaus and members of local Better Business Bureaus for their invaluable assistance:

- Steven Cole, President and CEO, Council of Better Business Bureaus
- Steve Cox, Vice President of Communications, Council of Better Business Bureaus
- Sheila Adkins, Director, Public Affairs, Council of Better Business Bureaus
- Ron Berry, Senior Vice President, Bureau Services Division, Council of Better Business Bureaus
- Steve Salter, Vice President, BBBOnLine
- Sally Munn, Vice President, Marketing & Membership Development, Council of Better Business Bureaus
- Fred Elsberry, President & CEO, BBB of Metro Atlanta, Athens, and Northeast Georgia
- Gary Almond, General Manager, BBB of Los Angeles County, Orange County, Riverside County, and San Bernardino County
- Tim Johnston, President & CEO, BBB of Northern Nevada
- Tricia Rossi, Operations Manager, BBB of Eastern Massachusetts, Maine, and Vermont
- Matthew Felling, President & CEO, BBB of Central and Northern Arizona
- James Baumhart, President & CEO, BBB of Chicago and Northern Illinois
- Kip Morse, President & General Manager, BBB of Central Ohio
- Katie Young, Director of Marketing & Communications, BBB of Alaska, Oregon, and Western Washington
- Charlie Mattingly, President & CEO, BBB of Louisville, Kentucky

Mard Naman would like to thank the following for their insight and expertise:

- Todd Cameron, BBB member, Subway franchise owner, and venture capitalist, Columbus, Ohio
- Peter Chase, Franchise and Business Attorney, Boston, Massachusetts
- Maurice Dussaq, BBB Executive Committee and Board of Directors member and owner of two FastSigns franchises, Reno, Nevada
- Dawn Eisenzimer, Director of New Franchise Development, Great Harvest Bread Company, Dillon, Montana
- Chuck Griffin, BBB member and owner of three Domino's Pizza restaurants, Santa Cruz, California
- Mario Herman, Franchise Attorney, Adamstown, Maryland
- Jon Jameson, President and CEO, MaggieMoo's Ice Cream and Treatery
- Michael Landry, Franchise Sales Director, Planet Beach Tanning and Day Spa, New Orleans, Louisiana
- Robert L. Purvin, Chairman and CEO, American Association of Franchisees and Dealers (AAFD), San Diego, California
- John Riggins, President, BBB of Fort Worth, Texas
- Roman Versch, President and Owner of Pet Depot franchise, Los Angeles, California
- Ellie Vogel, BBB member and founder of Franchise Finder, a franchise consultant firm, Boston, Massachusetts

Every member of The Planning Shop's extended team is dedicated to producing the highest quality products and brings a special talent that enables us to develop thorough, practical, helpful, and graphically appealing books and business tools:

- Rhonda Abrams, Founder and CEO
- Maggie Canon, Managing Editor
- Mireille Majoor, Editorial Project Manager
- Deborah Kaye, Director of Academic Sales
- Rosa Whitten, Office Manager
- Diana Van Winkle, Graphic Designer
- Mard Naman, Writer
- Kathryn Dean, Copyeditor and Indexer
- Bridgett Novak, Contributing Editor
- Arthur Wait, Design and Technology Consultant
- Cosmo, Chief Canine Companion

The latest business tips, trends, and insights...

...all in The Planning Shop's free monthly email newsletter!

Want to stay on top of the latest trends in marketing, sales, and management? Looking for tips and advice that make you more effective, competitive, and profitable? Check out The Planning Shop Report, a free email newsletter from Rhonda Abrams and The Planning Shop.

Sign up for *free* at www.PlanningShop.com

Grow Your Business with The Planning Shop!

We offer a full complement of books and tools to help you build your business **successfully**.

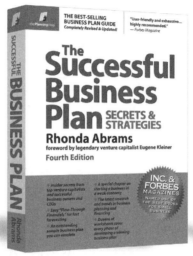

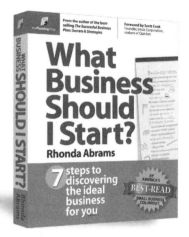

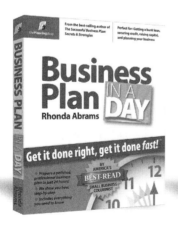

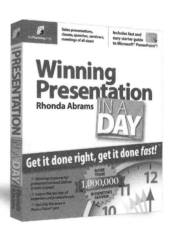

Ask your bookseller about these titles or visit www.PlanningShop.com

There's more where this book came from!

Better Business Bureau
Insider's Guide to Success
Starting an eBay Business

Are you thinking of starting an eBay business? Want to get more sales for your company? This thorough guide provides the keys to success, from choosing the right products and targeting the best eBay customers to understanding the technical aspects, creating listings that get attention, using pricing strategies, excelling at customer service, and much more.

Better Business Bureau
Insider's Guide to Success
Buying a Home

In the market for your first home or considering an investment property? This book is for you! Get the scoop on neighborhoods, schools, safety, and zoning. Find out what you need to know about inspections, escrow, closing, and legal issues. Includes a special section on checking out new home builders. Get your dream home at the best price!

Ask your bookseller about these other
Better Bus   Ides to Success
or fir   hop.com